THE BANBURY & CHELTENHAM RAILWAY

THE BANBURY & CHELTENHAM RAILWAY

VOLUME TWO

BY
WILLIAM HEMMINGS,
PAUL KARAU & CHRIS TURNER

J. H. MOSS

WILD SWAN PUBLICATIONS

ISBN 1 874103 89 5

FOR FRED WARREN
a 'Chippy' railwayman

GRADIENT PROFILE

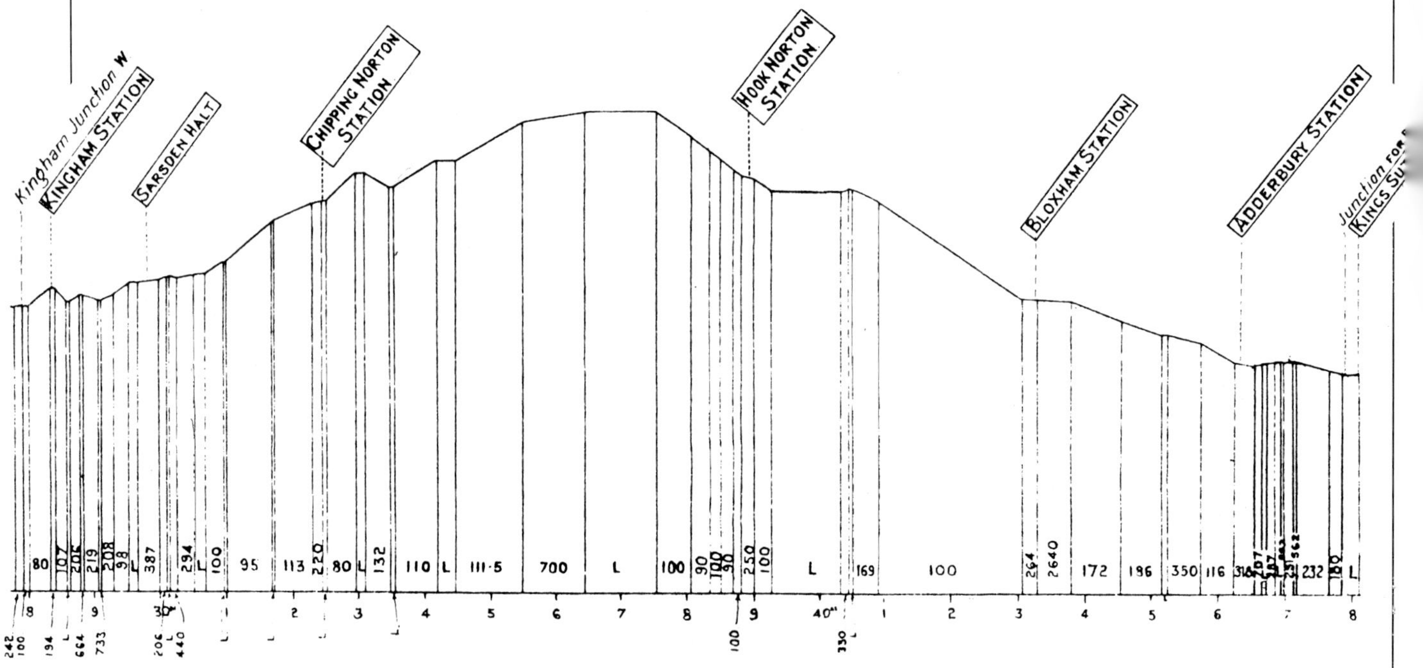

Designed by Paul Karau
Printed by Amadeus Press, Cleckheaton

Published by
WILD SWAN PUBLICATIONS LTD.
1-3 Hagbourne Road, Didcot, Oxon, OX11 8DP

J. H. MOSS

CONTENTS

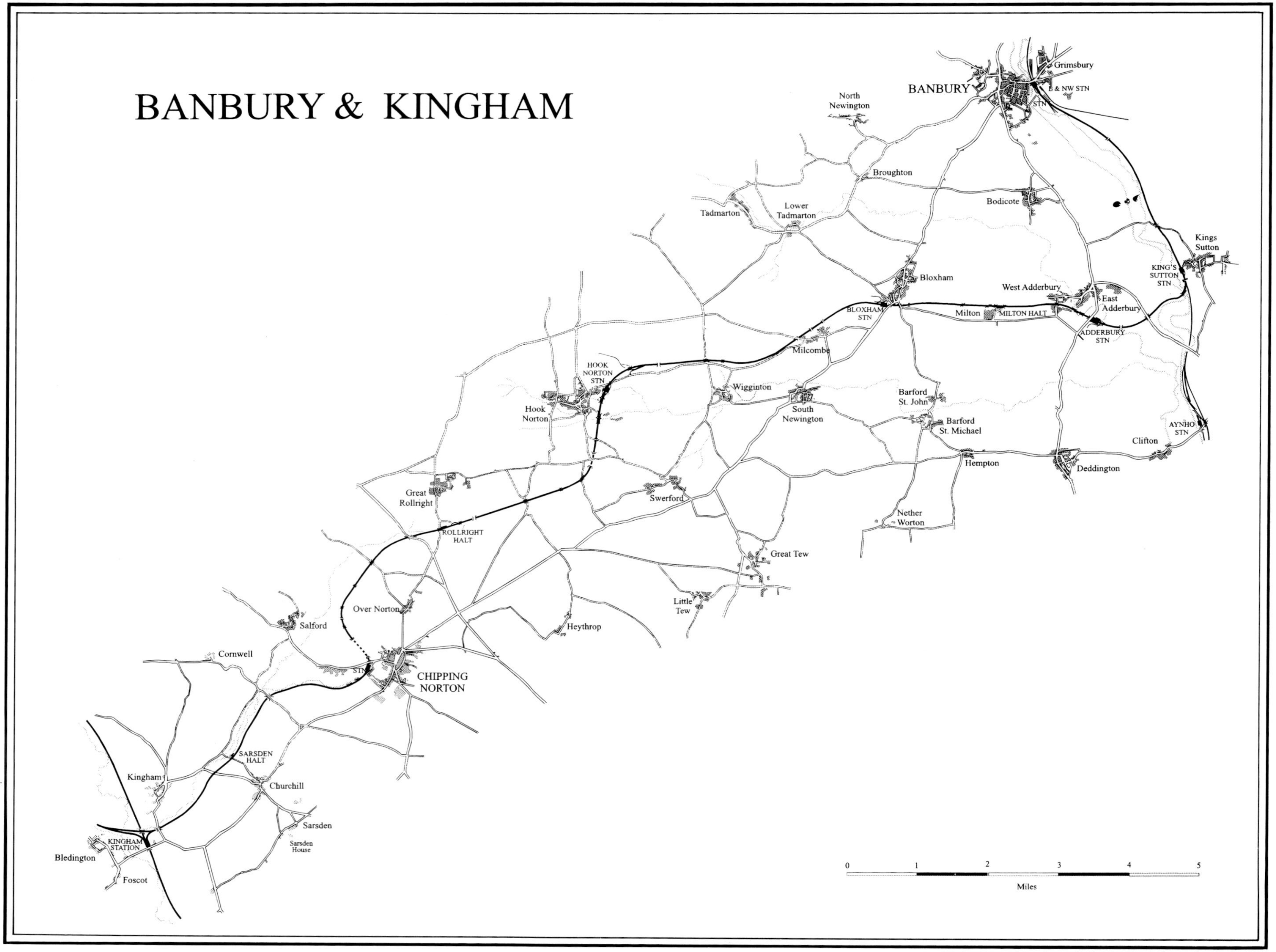
BANBURY & KINGHAM
BANBURY
Grimsbury
L & NW STN
STN
North Newington
Broughton
Bodicote
Tadmarton
Lower Tadmarton
Kings Sutton
KING'S SUTTON STN
Bloxham
West Adderbury
East Adderbury
BLOXHAM STN
Milton
MILTON HALT
ADDERBURY STN
Milcombe
HOOK NORTON STN
Hook Norton
Wigginton
South Newington
Barford St. John
Barford St. Michael
Clifton
AYNHO STN
Hempton
Deddington
Great Rollright
Swerford
Nether Worton
ROLLRIGHT HALT
Great Tew
Little Tew
Over Norton
Salford
Heythrop
Cornwell
STN
CHIPPING NORTON
SARSDEN HALT
Kingham
Churchill
Sarsden
Sarsden House
KINGHAM STATION
Bledington
Foscot
0
1
2
3
4
5
Miles

CHAPTER EIGHT

THE 6.22 a.m. BANBURY–KINGHAM AUTOCAR

A journey along the route in 1947

Banbury station forecourt on 13th August 1948. J. R. BATTS

IN the promise of the early morning sun, the tired old train shed at Banbury was in shadow, the cool interior contrasting sharply with the light reflecting from the platform surfaces outside. Part of the main buildings on the opposite platform caught the soft rays of the sun, which gave the faded cream paintwork a rich golden glow.

In the early postwar years, the sagging timbers of the 1850s structure, the indiscreet repairs, the tired and flat paintwork encrusted and ingrained with years of grime and smoke from the passing of thousands of trains, all betrayed its urgent need of attention.

As a matter of routine, the staff cleaned the windows, polished the door knobs, washed the floors and swept the platforms, but none of this disguised the years of neglect. The situation had come about through a much delayed ambitious scheme to radically rebuild the whole station in 1939, but the war had intervened. The goods depot to the south of the station had been replaced by a large, brick-built structure, whilst the road bridge to the north had been provided with an additional span to accommodate the proposed new layout. But between them, the old station sat, untouched and neglected. Now even the glazing was missing from the roof, allowing the rain and snow to penetrate the very heart of the station.

Notwithstanding this sad state of affairs, there was a strange peace inside, which could readily inspire a reverence for the past, in some ways not unlike that found in an old church that had witnessed centuries of ritual. A handful of posters on the walls offered the prospect of holidays at idealised locations or the promise of branded products. These bold visual statements of a modern generation stamping its identity irreverently on the timelocked Victorian interior were peculiarly reassuring – a promise for the future.

However, even at this time of the morning, the peace was broken by two passengers arriving through the main entrance on the down platform and making their way up the steps and over the wooden boards of the footbridge to reach the up platform. The opening and closing of doors drew attention to staff going about their duties, sometimes unwittingly disturbing one or two of the scavenging pigeons that strutted up and down the platforms, causing the sound of beating wings to echo through the interior.

The station would not come alive until later when the refreshment room and book stall were opened to cater for the regular commuters and other travellers. Even so, the scent of fresh newsprint was still apparent in the cocktail of smells in the train shed, bundles of newspapers having arrived earlier on a train from Reading. The hamper of dirty

A glimpse of the down platform from beneath the footbridge on 25th July 1949. NATIONAL RAILWAY MUSEUM

The footbridge and the lofty roof of the interior of Banbury station, revealing the fine carpentry expressed in the roof trusses. The Kingham bay was just outside on the left. 25th July 1949. NATIONAL RAILWAY MUSEUM

crockery outside the refreshment room doors bore the smell of stale milk, disinfectant lingered in the air near the lavatories, whilst warm paraffin vapour from the hand lamps, spare tail lamps, etc., teased the senses ... and then there was the stack of fish boxes.

The Kingham auto-car was stabled outside in the sun, against the buffer-stops of the south end bay behind the up platform. It had been put there the night before by the station pilot which had also put the empty stock for the 5.55 a.m. workmen's train to Cowley in front of it.

Since the departure of the 5.55, the little Collett 48XX tank engine had come over from the shed and been coupled onto the coach and was now gently simmering there.

The tranquil atmosphere inside the train shed was rudely disturbed again, this time by the harsh rumble of the four-wheel trolley, which the early-turn porter dragged along the platform, laden with an assortment of newspapers, parcels and fish boxes, all quivering and jolting from the vibration of its solid little unsprung wheels.

At various times this first train to Kingham had a fish van in tow, but today the fish boxes were being taken in the luggage compartment of the autocar, stacked neatly on a special 4ft square metal tray laid inside to protect the floor from the melting ice, etc.

The drab and faded chocolate and cream paintwork on the sides of the autocar was clean and even though it was so obviously patina ingrained, there was still a slight sheen to the finish.

Stepping through the central doorway, passengers were faced with an instant decision of whether to go into the saloon to the right of them where transfers on the window declared that smoking was allowed, or the one to the left, towards the back, where the air might be fresher.

Turning left, the seats nearest to the centre vestibule were longitudinally placed along each side, followed by bays of so-called 'walkover seating' where the seat backs were pivoted to give travellers the choice of direction they wished to face.

The longitudinal seats allowed spontaneous access to the opening droplights of the centre vestibule doors for a better view without disturbing the other passengers.

While the loading of the guard's compartment was being completed and departure time grew ever nearer, there was time to gaze around. The windows, although commendably clean, did not bear close inspection where the glass joined

The south end of the station on Monday, 21st August 1950, with an auto-coach in the Kingham bay on the right. R. F. ROBERTS

This bay platform was used by both the Kingham and Princes Risborough auto-trains. Which service No. 1401 and its single auto-trailer had been rostered for on this occasion is not recorded. The picture was taken from a train alongside the up main platform.
A. W. V. MACE, CTY. MILEPOST 92½

the dark varnished wood surrounds. But then the very sweeping out of the interior produced a tidy-looking floor, but significantly added to the dust which inevitably settled in every nook and cranny, especially in the coarse green rep corded fabric of the upholstery which, if disturbed by anyone brushing off their seat, produced a cloud of tiny particles which would hover in the sunlight, contributing to the ultra-dry dusty odour once so familiar to regular users of all forms of public transport.

Former staff from this time recall three regular travellers on this train, one apparently employed by an upholsterer at Hook Norton whilst the other two were workers at Bliss Mill, Chipping Norton. The guard, whose compartment was right behind the engine, looked at his pocket watch and at 6.22 a.m. just raised his arm to acknowledge the tip from the porter. Then, with his flag still furled, he simply turned around and with the smallest gesture gave the 'Right away' to the driver, who gave a touch on the whistle, and without any fuss, the train was on the move.

As the train pulled away along the bay platform, it gradually accelerated, the lamp posts passing by the window more quickly as the speed increased. Just past the platform end, the track converged with the up main, the wheels of the coach clattering over the pointwork as the train joined it. The goods shed was on the right whilst, on the left, numerous strings of wagons prevented any glimpse of the neighbouring LMS (ex-LNWR) terminus. Not until the gasworks situated on the boundary between the two railway companies had been passed was it possible to see the LMS approach lines coming in from across the fields.

The track running immediately below the left-hand windows of the coach was the up goods loop whilst to our right, beyond the down goods loop, were more sidings and the busy GWR engine shed where a number of locos were evidently being prepared for the day ahead. Lowering the right-hand window in the centre vestibule of the coach and leaning out slightly, the four tracks could be seen stretching ahead towards the three-arch bridge at Franklow Knob nearly a mile away, and the sound of the loco was more obvious with its vacuum pump spitting quickly as the crossheads shuffled rapidly backwards and forwards between the frames. The train was now moving effortlessly along the main line with the coach wheels clicking rhythmically over the rail joints on a barely perceptible down grade of 1 in 1077 at a speed of about 40 mph. This rhythm was accompanied by a gentle creaking and groaning from beneath the floor of the coach and every now and then, there was just the odd trace of the smell of steam and hot oil wafting past the window; the passing telegraph poles with their endless swooping wires added to the sense of speed.

After passing under the bridge, the lines curved gently to the right and some two miles from Banbury were the end of

The approach to King's Sutton from the north, looking back towards Banbury from the Twyford Road bridge. The three-arch structure in in the background carried the lane to Twyford Farm. H. J. STRETTON WARD

Looking in the opposite direction towards King's Sutton from the Twyford Road bridge. The railway here begins its descent through the flood plain of the River Cherwell. The elegant spire of King's Sutton church, on high ground east of the river, can be seen in the left distance. H. J. STRETTON WARD

the goods loops and Astrop Sidings Signal Box. These loops sometimes held queues of four or five goods trains awaiting their turn for line occupation.

Now just the double track continued into a cutting, past Twyford Mill on the right and under an accommodation bridge carrying a private lane to King's Sutton Lodge, then another bearing the Banbury to King's Sutton road.

From here the line was carried across the broad, lush flood plain of the River Cherwell on a low embankment and as the distinctive tall chimneys of King's Sutton station grew closer, the train began to slow, finally coming to rest alongside the up platform.

For the discerning passenger, casting an eye around the station was no anticlimax; the chimneys heralded great promise and the detailing of the red brick structure which supported them was exquisite, from the dressed stone quoins and cills to the finely worked chimney stacks it was a joy to behold. Even its far simpler counterpart on the opposite

A view of the final approach to King's Sutton station, as seen from the footplate of 54XX 0–6–0PT No. 5407 propelling a Kingham to Banbury auto-trailer along the down main on 25th June 1951. On 17th April 1875, a herd of young horses escaped from Banbury station after being unloaded, and galloped towards King's Sutton. They dodged a gang of platelayers and avoided the 11.14 a.m. train standing in King's Sutton station before being rounded up there. J. R. BATTS

The charm of King's Sutton station is clear to see in this view looking north towards Banbury on a bright summer day in the 1950s. The somewhat austere footbridge added c.1909 did not quite match the attention to detail expressed in the station buildings.
LENS OF SUTTON

platform exuded the love and enthusiasm of its architect who, all those years ago, so obviously wanted to create so much more than a functional shell.

The village of King's Sutton with its narrow picture-book streets sprawls off to the east, and the imposing and extensive row of tall chestnut trees which still line the eastern boundary of the goods yard today, ensured that the gently rolling pastures behind the church and manor house were spared the view and sounds of the busy main line.

In contrast, the timeless prospect over the water meadows to the west was open and enticing, especially to local fishermen, among whom was the King's Sutton station master Leonard Almond.

Without any passengers boarding the Kingham train here, the 'auto' set off again, the lowered arm of the bracket signal against the 'black bridge' ahead reading to the right for the junction beyond. It accelerated past the goods yard, which at this time of the day was still deserted, then after passing

No. 7900 Saint Peter's Hall *passing King's Sutton signal box with the 10.0 a.m. Bradford (Exchange) to Poole on 8th September 1962. 'Black Bridge' carried a lane to Sydenham Farm.*
R. A. F. PURYER

King's Sutton Junction on 19th May 1963 with the B&CD line to Kingham curving away to the right. The field to the right of the junction was the site of a paint factory which had existed there during the 19th century. Villagers still discovered traces of paint in the banks of the River Cherwell up to the 1920s. The position of the original King's Sutton branch signal box, demolished when Adderbury signal box was replaced in 1906, was positioned near the outer home signal. The Cherwell flood arches are just visible at the far right. M. HALE

A series of brick flood arches carried the railway across the flood plain of the River Cherwell, followed by a bridge spanning the River Cherwell and the Oxford Canal. The view on the right shows the span over the canal.
A. W. DONALDSON

beneath the 'black bridge', which carried a farm track across the entire width of the site, it was possible to catch a brief glimpse of King's Sutton Junction Signal Box, which stood coyly in the shadows. There was a 20 mph speed restriction for trains routed over the right-hand curve at the commencement of the Banbury & Cheltenham route, the curvature being sharp enough to cause the wheel flanges to squeal in protest after their easy ride on the main line.

Even here in the low-lying landscape the situation was special for this was no unmemorable length of railway track but an enchanting corner where the long-awaited Banbury & Cheltenham Direct was borne across the rustic water meadow on attractive, low, brick flood arches, closely followed by more brick arches over the River Cherwell and a single plate girder span over the Oxford Canal.

Fireman Stanley Cowley recalled the sight of kingfishers here whilst fireman Michael Clifton recalls the regular sighting of a Little Owl in the remains of one of the ironstone kilns nearby.

Such beginnings offered a promise of the route beckoning ahead and even today the magical beauty of the area is never a disappointment. Leaving the main line confidently striding through the Cherwell Valley, the sweeping curve of the Banbury & Cheltenham ushered travellers through what might be thought of as a sort of gateway to the southern fringes of the ironstone kingdom. With views at times reminiscent of Devonshire, the journey through this unassuming area, overlooked by all but the most seasoned traveller, had a truly unique feel. The well-farmed landscape had been used and scarred through industrial necessity, yet in only a few decades the machinery had come and gone and a rural peace now endures again in the working communities. Nature has reclaimed the workings and what little evidence remains only adds to the mysteries of the timeless landscape.

This was no easy route for heavy traffic, the climb away from the main line at 1 in 180 beginning an ascent which continued with little respite for the next ten miles to the summit beyond Hook Norton.

From the left-hand side of the coach, passengers could see the overgrown earthworks of the abandoned southern loop which would have given direct running to and from the Oxford direction and the Bicester cut-off. The canal was also in view, the line following its course for some half a mile before it veered away to the south, whilst on the opposite side were the derelict remains of the long-abandoned Sydenham and Adderbury ironstone workings. Continuing a

The Banbury and Cheltenham lines between King's Sutton and Adderbury were doubled in 1906. This view, across the valley of the Sor Brook, shows the gentle westward sweep of the line as it passed under the A41 Aynho road, one mile east of King's Sutton station.
H. J. STRETTON WARD

Adderbury station, looking towards Bloxham with the start of the single-line section beyond the over-bridge in the distance.
E. T. GILL
CTY. R. K. BLENCOWE

south-westerly course, the line entered a cutting, bridged by the A441 trunk road, then, curving gently right towards Adderbury, was borne by a short embankment leading to another cutting bridged by a farm track.

Having shut off steam by now, the driver let the train coast down the 1 in 858 gradient which prevailed throughout the remainder of the long curve towards the extremities of Adderbury station, a long, low embankment along this stretch providing panoramic views over gentle farmland before passing the gaunt-looking goods shed which, in its commanding position above the surrounding fields, dominated the elevated earthworks at the east end of the station. When compared with equivalent structures on other railways, it was no larger than might have been expected but its taller proportions, two-storey office extension and lack of embellishment, emphasised its rather stark, almost brooding image. As will be seen, this fascinating design was repeated at Bloxham and Hook Norton.

The train came to a stand in the platform where it was greeted by the early-turn signalman. The double line ended here, so he handed to the driver the train staff which was his authority to enter the single-line section ahead.

As the early-turn signalman was the only member of staff on duty at this time, it fell to him to unlock the station, book any passengers for the first train and carry out platform duties. With the guard's help, he therefore unloaded the newspapers, parcels and a box of fish from the guard's van onto a platform trolley.

Through the right-hand windows the main station building was visible on the opposite platform whilst ahead, both platforms were flanked with tall conifers. These had been planted at the request of the owner of Adderbury House to screen the railway from view. Looking through the trees and beyond the platform fence, from the left-hand windows revealed the extensive premises of Twyford's Seeds which were served by a private siding. During the war, this had been an aluminium reclamation factory, but more of this later. With two more passengers on board and after exchanging pleasantries with the signalman, the guard signalled the 'Right Away' to the fireman who was looking back from his side of the cab, and the train was off.

The station at Adderbury was situated on a gradient of 1 in 330, and beyond the bridge carrying the Deddington road over the line, the gradient steepened to 1 in 116 through Berry Hill cutting. For the next mile the sound of the trackbed altered somewhat as it passed over the section of steel-sleepered track. This was laid during the 1930s as a replacement for the wooden sleepers which had rotted largely due to activity of ants. The embankment which followed Berry Hill carried the line over the flood plain of the Sor Brook which was crossed three times on brick arch bridges. At this point the formation was about 25ft above its surroundings with a glorious panorama over East Adderbury and the spire of St. Mary's church to the fore.

After leaving Adderbury, the line passed below the Deddington road bridge and became single for the first time, entering the deep Berry Hill cutting. Close to this point, at Hilly Fields, Adderbury signalman George Sandalls kept a smallholding. Such was his enthusiasm for animal husbandry that fellow railwaymen nicknamed him 'Farmer One Cow'. In fact he owned two, as well as an assortment of other livestock. H. J. STRETTON WARD

The second of three brick arched bridges carrying the railway over the Sor Brook, Adderbury, with Adderbury Mill beyond. The poor quality of the brickwork is evident in this c.1907 view. The two bridges here suffered extensively during construction of the railway in the mid 1870s. COLLECTION J. FOX

The village of West Adderbury, on the west side of the Sor Brook was bisected by the embankment, with bridges over Tanners Lane and Horn Hill maintaining the connection between the severed parts which were overlooked from both sides of the carriage.

The closeness of the cottages gave the impression that the railway was making a rude and unwanted intrusion. Norman Davis, who recalled his childhood at the nearby Dog and Partridge public house in Tanners Lane, recalled that the passing of the 'Ports to Ports' express and ironstone trains "made the building shake".

The line now headed due west through open countryside, parallel to the Adderbury to Bloxham road. About a mile further on, an embankment maintained the course immedi-

West Adderbury was a community literally bisected by the railway. This view shows the bridge carrying the railway over Tanner's Lane, with the Dog and Partridge public house seen through the arch. The passing of heavy trains made the building shake. COLLECTION A. W. DONALDSON

The second of the two bridges at West Adderbury spanned Horn Hill Road. This view was taken looking north towards Cross Hill. COLLECTION A. W. DONALDSON

View of Horn Hill Road, looking south. COLLECTION J. FOX

The view east from the top of the Horn Hill Road bridge, with the Adderbury up distant and the parapets of the Tanner's Hill road bridge in the distance. The embankments were rented to the villagers whose land bordered the railway, mainly in Horn Hill Road. Several had pieces of land. The Lynes family kept goats on the allotment, and paid 7s 6d per year to the Great Western for the lease. Others planted vegetables. COLLECTION A. W. DONALDSON

Photos of Milton Halt are hard to come by. This corner of a family picture shows the back of the platform and pagoda shelter perched on the side of the embankment viewed from the garden of Manor Farm. CTY. JON & DIANA ADAMS

No. 5404 with a Banbury to Kingham auto passing through Barford cutting, just east of Bloxham station. R. H. G. SIMPSON

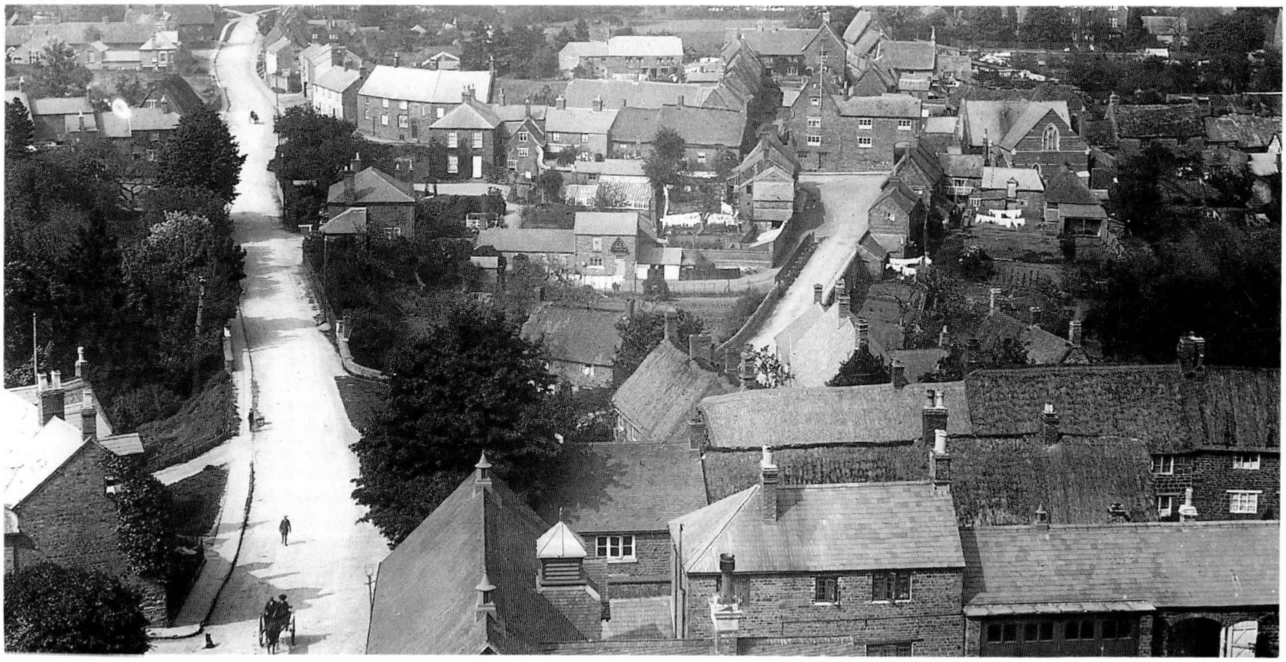

Bloxham village, viewed from the tall spire of St. Mary's Church. Businesses regularly using Bloxham station feature in this view, including Tom Simpson's post office and chemist, in Virginia House (far left foreground), Emma Coleman's carrier's business in Merivales Lane (right foreground) and All Saints School, whose pupils' luggage was delivered by rail at the beginning and end of each term (top left).
Centre for Oxfordshire Studies, WESTGATE LIBRARY

ately to the north of the tiny village of Milton which was served by a halt whose wooden platform was constructed above the community on the south side of the embankment.

The train passed the gardens of Manor Farm to the south, approaching with caution until it was apparent that there wasn't anyone waiting on the platform, then the driver opened up again to regain momentum and continue towards Bloxham over gradients of 1 in 350, 1 in 186 and 1 in 172.

To the left passengers could look down over the stone dwellings straggling along Tinkers Lane which was crossed by a red-brick arch bridge, wide enough to span a main road. In the early 1880s this lane had been designated as part of a main road planned from Barford St. John to Banbury via Bloxham Grove, but this never materialised and the lane simply petered out under the bridge with only footpaths to Wayhouse Farm and Bloxham Grove continuing beyond.

Not far past Milton, a derelict engine shed to the right marked the site where sidings once served the Bloxham Ironworks Co. which had closed in 1929. Shortly after was the smallholding of Brickhouse Farm, which was tight to the boundary on the south side.

Only on the final approach to Bloxham did the gradient ease to 1 in 2,640. The driver shut off through a cutting which took the line past the southern tip of the village, crossed by a single-arch bridge carrying the road to Barford St. John, a slender lattice footbridge maintaining a right of way and a plate girder bridge carrying the A361 Banbury to Chipping Norton road.

The train drew up alongside the down platform where the signalman exchanged single-line staffs with the engine crew, then, while two more passengers climbed aboard, he drew

A peaceful scene at Bloxham station. The vegetable allotments which replaced Herbert Lloyd's station gardens show the careful attention given by the station staff, Bert Lane, Harold Hall and Fred Watson. D. THOMPSON

the platform trolley alongside the guard's van in order to load the travelling safe, then take delivery of Bloxham's allocation of newspapers, parcels and fish boxes.

As with Adderbury, the main building was on the opposite platform, and the accommodation alongside on the down platform was also confined to another brick-built waiting room with a sloping canopy roof. Although a few conifers had been planted along the platforms during the Great War by one-time station master Frank Coppage, they certainly did not compare with Adderbury, and at Bloxham there was a largely uninterrupted view to the south across the village sports ground.

The station was situated on a 1 in 264 gradient and just ahead this steepened to 1 in 100 so the loco accelerated past the goods yard with more vigour as it left Bloxham. The line

This Frank Packer photograph reveals the beautiful rural scene between Bloxham and Hook Norton, showing the village of Milcombe from the slopes of Fern Hill, looking south. The railway ran left to right (east to west) through the cutting in the foreground The road winding through the centre of the view is Paradise Lane, at the end of which were the three thatched cottages seen in the centre of the picture. Bloxham ganger Fred Nash lived in the upper building (now demolished). Edith ('Queenie') White lived in the lower cottage. She was often available to brew up a pot of tea for the permanent way staff as they patrolled the length.

F. R. PACKER, CTY. B. WOODWARD

curved to the left beyond the station to head south-westwards, squeezing between the lower slope of Fern Hill and the northern edge of the village of Milcombe, although the proximity of the village was not apparent from the train as the cutting here was deep enough to hide the scene from view.

The cutting was spanned by two bridges bearing farm tracks and, past the village, another bridge carrying the road to Wigginton Heath.

After this the line ran through sloping farmland which fell towards the south, the climb easing to 1 in 169 for about half a mile before reaching an interim summit beyond which the line fell at 1 in 330 for just over a furlong, then levelled out for a mile alongside Council Hill.

The top of Milcombe bank was marked by a stop board applying to loose-coupled trains travelling in the opposite direction. Here up goods trains without continuous brakes were obliged to come to a stand in order for the guard to pin

down sufficient brakes to help keep the train under control on the long descent ahead.

Glebe Farm, on the north side of the Hook Norton road, marked the position of the stop board. Here, where the track was level with the surrounding land, Tom Powell, tenant of the farm, recalls the frequently occurring sound of wheels slipping on the greasy rails in wet weather as drivers sanded for grip to pull away against the brakes from a standing start. He remembers the story of a fully loaded goods train returning from Kingham to Banbury which overran the stop board. "It never stopped but ran down and overshot the points at Bloxham and derailed."

After the steep climb, the driver of the auto train eased off and the sound of the exhaust was barely audible for the level stretch along an embankment, pierced by a bridge over the road linking the village of Wigginton with Wigginton Heath.

From the left-hand window, the road veered away gradually to avoid the slope of the hill whilst the railway, then level with the surrounding farmland, maintained its heading by means of a cutting which the rising ground to the north caused to be much deeper on the right. On the other side of a bridge carrying another farm lane over the cutting, were sidings serving the extensive but now closed Brymbo ironstone works where ironstone from the local quarries was loaded for despatch to the Brymbo Steelworks near Wrexham. From the left-hand window it was possible to see the now disused sidings making their gradual descent to four

Hook Norton station and signal box, looking west towards Chipping Norton.
LENS OF SUTTON

The Railway Hotel was situated in the triangle of land formed by the Milcombe Road, the railway and the station approach (out of view to the right). The hotel was a large brick structure and in the 1920s was tenanted by Mr. and Mrs. Andrews. The building was frequented by railway staff. The tenants' daughter, Doris Andrews, married Hook Norton signalman Jimmy Fairbrother in 1922. The signal box is just visible to the right of the hotel.
OXFORDSHIRE CENTRAL LIBRARY

The alignment of the railway through Hook Norton turned from west to south in order to carry it across the two viaducts spanning tributaries of the River Swere. J. H. MOSS

calcinating kilns which were still standing at this time, but would be demolished the following year.

From here the line began to swing left on a long arc, which would eventually take it on a virtually southbound heading across the valley between the village of Hook Norton and South Hill. This distinctive 'S' formation of the alignment was an enduring feature of the Banbury & Cheltenham Railway, making the route readily identifiable on even small-scale maps. The steep ascent resumed again on the curve with a 1 in 100 gradient for a quarter of a mile along embankment where a bridge over another farm lane had also accommodated the narrow-gauge rails of one of the quarry tramways. The auto-train made a chirpy enough approach up the 1 in 100, shutting off a short distance before the Hook Norton to Bloxham road was crossed on the skew by a plate girder bridge. This structure carried both up and down tracks of the station crossing loop and a trailing connection to the ironstone sidings behind the down platform. To the right the line overlooked the Station Hotel situated on the roadside below, whilst not far from the end of the up platform, the signal box and the main station building came into view. Once again the train came to a stand alongside one of the simple brick-built waiting rooms with its sloping canopy roof and was met by the signalman who exchanged single-line staffs with the crew of the engine. For much of the day these single-line staff exchanges were either carried out on the boarded crossings near each signal box or by using the lineside exchange apparatus provided for the purpose, but as the signalmen were carrying out the station work at this time of day, they had to be on the platform anyway.

The passengers, two men and three women, waiting on the platform were workers for Bliss Mill at Chipping Norton. In the time-honoured way in which passengers like to find their own spaces in a railway carriage, the growing number of occupants were now spreading throughout the sunlit interior and the emptiness of the train at the beginning of the journey was no longer so apparent. In the meantime, while the guard and signalman were unloading the newspapers, parcels and fish boxes for the village onto a trolley, it was possible to gaze out of the window through the iron railings running along the back of the platform and look over the rolling hillsides on the opposite side of the valley in anticipation of the views ahead.

The entire station was situated on an extensive embankment, on a curve, on a gradient of 1 in 250. Furthermore, to add to the drama of this spectacular setting, as the train exchanged the security of the solid ground for the deck of the first of the five lofty lattice girder spans, the gradient of the line steepened to 1 in 100 across the 188-yard structure.

The little auto-tank with its single coach might have barked a certain amount as it accelerated out of the station, gaining speed for the climb ahead (depending on the skill of the driver) but the load was nominal, especially compared to a heavily laden goods train attempting to gain momentum on the 1 in 100 in order to cope with the greasy rails through the tunnel ahead. In these circumstances the 20 mph speed restriction signs for the viaduct must have seemed ironic, to say the least.

Even local passengers intimately familiar with their surroundings were frequently drawn to the view over the tree tops from either side of the viaducts but a first-time traveller over this stretch would have been forgiven for hurriedly leaving their seat to reach the open droplight of the centre vestibule door in order to lean out and take in the spectacular view from this 90ft high vantage point.

The railway in its landscape. Hook Norton village forms the backdrop to this view of the Banbury & Cheltenham Railway, looking north-west from the lower slopes of South Hill. Centre for Oxfordshire Studies, WESTGATE LIBRARY

A closer view of No. 2 viaduct. F. R. PACKER

To the west, the sun was just beginning to warm the mix of thatch, slate and stone-tiled roofs of the higgledy-piggledy cottages lining the web of narrow roads and lanes criss-crossing the green hillside. Situated on the western edge of the ironstone belt, the sprawling village of Hook Norton is all the more alluring through the appeal of the time-mellowed deep yellow ochre and brownish deep mustard colour stonework which looks so warm, particularly in the orange glow of a setting sun.

Today it would be easy to overlook the industrial nature of the Hook Norton landscape which for decades was scarred with tramways, kilns and all manner of buildings and equipment associated with the working of the ironstone quarries, calcination and the despatch of the ore which had been made possible by the coming of the railway. However, this was a relatively shortlived era and by the time of the journey described the evidence was already fading as nature reclaimed the hillsides and tranquillity returned.

The experience of leaning out of the gently swaying coach, with so little between oneself and the huge drop below, was quite unnerving, but for those that did there was comfort in the knowledge that surely thousands of trains had passed this way safely enough over the years without incident.

At the end of the first viaduct the gradient steepened to 1 in 90 for a furlong or more over an embankment before the second more extensive viaduct, whose eight spans carried the line for 296 yards at 1 in 100.

The up fixed distant for Hook Norton and the illuminated 20 mph speed restriction indicator which applied to the viaducts ahead. Hook Norton station can just be seen in the distance.

J. H. RUSSELL

Two views of the Swerford road bridge spanning the cutting into South Hill, where the line was on a rising 1 in 100 gradient towards the tunnel.
R. H. G. SIMPSON
and J. H. RUSSELL

Beyond the second viaduct another embankment reached out from the hillside to carry the line past the site of more ironstone sidings on the left. A brick arch bridge carrying the Hook Norton to Swerford road spanned the beginning of a shadowed cutting which deepened as the line, now climbing at 1 in 100, plunged ever deeper into the northern slope of South Hill before the sound of the engine whistle indicated that the little auto-train was about to enter the unwelcoming black confines of the small-bore tunnel.

As if the gradient was not difficult enough in itself, the course of the line changed inside so the track was also on a curve throughout the 418-yard bore which former enginemen recall as damp – "The rails were always wet". Drivers of heavy trains gave the wheels "a shake of sand" in the hope of avoiding wheelslip which would slow momentum and all too easily bring a heavy train down to a crawl. With limited clearance inside the tunnel, the exhaust from the chimney would hammer the roof with a deafening blast and the smoke and fumes rapidly filled the air space.

The crew could soon find themselves struggling for air in the cab and some recall that if this happened, holding coats over their heads, they quickly pulled up the inspection plate in the floor, in front of the firebox doors, to breathe the air from under the loco. Former Banbury engineman Stan Cowley recalls crouching down near slightly opened firehole doors while going through the tunnel, and that when Eric Simms was on the footplate he put a corn bag over his head – "collared from the goods department at Banbury". It is

The northern approach to Hook Norton tunnel. Originally planned as an open excavation, at its maximum depth the cutting reached some 76 feet. The workings at Hook Norton accounted for considerable loss of life. R. H. G. SIMPSON

A closer view of the northern portal of Hook Norton tunnel. J. H. RUSSELL

Upon leaving the southern portal of Hook Norton tunnel, the line began to resume its original westerly direction. The retaining walls were built to prevent the cutting sides slipping. This was a constant bugbear for the Banbury & Cheltenham Railway, for it was formed in clay. George Allen, who lived at Coldharbour Farm nearby, recalled the villagers' disinterested response to the problem and said "You could very often hear somebody say 'Oh there's another slip by Hooky again'. They used to have these gangs of old navvies come up there with wheelbarrows and shovels and move all this stuff off. Sometimes it would hold the trains up." Bert Field was a member of the Kingham permanent way gang which was sometimes called upon to help. He said "We had to do a lot of work there because the clay kept slipping, just at the mouth of the tunnel. We had to dig out all the clay. All the gangs mixed in together and we used to get there about 5 o'clock in the morning and spend the whole day digging out. We'd cut five to six-foot channels in the bank both sides. Then we put these big blocks in to stop it from slipping." These came with the train. Bert recalled engineering works in the tunnel itself. "There was always a lookout man so that whatever work was being done inside, a whistle was blown (if a train was coming) and everybody had to get clear. Of course, there were manholes in the tunnel so you could just stand up against the wall. But if ever there was any work being done with an engine inside (on a Sunday), you had to go outside the tunnel when they stoked it or you'd have been choked." J. R. BATTS

Rollright siding, looking north-east. At the time of this photograph, Charlie Cranmer was the Rollright porter. In this quiet upland region of the upper Swere valley, it was possible to hear the hooters of both the Brymbo Works at Hook Norton and the Bliss Mill at Chipping Norton. Brymbo used to go at 7.0 a.m, 12.0 noon, 1.0 p.m. restart and 5.0 p.m. Local people timed their watches by the two hooters.
C. F. D. WHETMATH

hardly surprising that drivers of goods trains did their utmost to get some sort of run at the tunnel in order to avoid problems.

Whilst the 5ft 2in wheels of the auto-tank might well show signs of a minor slip, there was normally no problem in climbing steadily through the tunnel, and the 'car' was soon out into the morning sunlight again, in a cutting, with the line still curving to the right to regain a more westerly course.

Just past the end of the cutting, the summit at the end of the barely relenting climb from King's Sutton was reached.

After passing over a small bridge spanning a minor lane, known as Cow Lane, the line continued on a level embankment and was soon on a straight course across the gentle sloping fields following the course of the little River Swere. The highest bridge on the Banbury to Kingham route spanned an accommodation track linking a farmer's fields, then after bridging the Chipping Norton to Hook Norton road, here known as 'The Walk', the line began a long descent to Chipping Norton, the first mile at 1 in 700 including a shallow cutting bridged by a farm lane but otherwise more or less level with the surrounding fields. This was a quiet location, some 560ft above sea level, home to scattered farms with unusual names like Duckpool Farm, Coltscombe and Coldharbour.

The ironstone belt was left behind at Hook Norton and from here onwards the paler creamy-grey hue of Oxfordshire limestone is apparent as the local building material.

The train slowed as it neared the unremarkable and remote Rollright Siding which passed the window on the right, and came to a stand alongside the sleeper-built platform at Rollright Halt. This was perched on the northern side of the embankment again on the right, just short of the Great Rollright road.

Rollright Halt and 'pagoda' shed. The fir trees screening the view of Rollright siding can be seen in the distance.
LENS OF SUTTON

There was no member of staff here until later on but, in any case, the three women passengers waiting to board here were workers for Bliss Mill and held season tickets. With the spacing of passengers throughout the coach, there were lots of empty seats but not an overwhelming choice of clear areas of seating for the group of three women, not that it would have mattered anyway for their brief journey.

The train was soon off again, the engine starting away easily down the 1 in 112 gradient and passing over the plate girder bridge spanning the Great Rollright road. The village was some half-mile away, further up the hill to the north.

A short distance further on, the line entered a cutting which effectively carried the railway into a different water-

View north through an occupation overbridge, close to the derelict farm buildings of Hillside. The broad sweep of the railway at this location overlooks the wide valley across to the village of Salford 1½ miles west. Beyond could be seen the brooding range of hills and the narrow path of Golden Lane leading up to the prehistoric trading route called the Jurassic Way.

J. H. RUSSELL

The Banbury & Cheltenham Railway continued its broad left-hand sweep into the spur of hills west of Chipping Norton, only straightening as it reached the tunnel that would take it into the valley below the town. The signal was the Chipping Norton down distant.

J. H. RUSSELL

shed, the streams feeding the River Evenlode seven miles to the west. A skewbridge carried the A34 Oxford to Stratford road over the cutting and was memorable for being faced with blue engineering brick on its eastern face and red flettons on the opposite side. From here the line started to bear round to the left and levelled out for quarter of a mile on an embankment which incorporated a bridge over the Long Compton to Over Norton road at Choicehill Farm.

Still bearing left and following the 500ft contour around the base of the Over Norton Hill, the falling gradient resumed at 1 in 110 on nearly three-quarters of a mile of embankment, levelled out for barely a furlong, then curving even more severely to the left, headed 90 degrees away from the valley. It was here that the trackbed is said to have been formed with clinker in order to provide protection from the effects of ground water under the line. Climbing at 1 in 132 through a brief cutting spanned by a farm track, the line then levelled out for a short embankment, immediately followed by a short shaded cutting leading directly into the dark 715 yard curving bore. Not only did the heading change inside but there was also a gradient of 1 in 80 falling towards Chipping Norton and, as if to test their skills, crews recall that, just like Hook Norton, it was wet inside. Unfitted goods trains had to descend through the tunnel with particu-

J. H. RUSSELL

A Banbury–Kingham goods train about to enter Chipping Norton tunnel. All these photographs were taken on a late summer afternoon in 1947. In the stretch of line between the north portal of the tunnel and the Choicehill bridge, rabbits abounded. The many duties carried out by the permanent way department included keeping the rabbit population down. Officially, this involved dispensing a poison called Cybmac through a machine into the burrows and then backfilling with earth. However, sub-ganger George Slatter was fond of rabbit pie so instead he set snares all along the line to beyond Rollright Halt. George Slatter frequently took his son Horace (who became a Kingham engineman in the 1950s) along on Sunday mornings when it was quiet, to snare the rabbits. He often let Horace drive the 'Buda pup', a small motorised trolley capable of carrying two people. As he explained, "He'd say to me, 'Stop up here'. I would stop, pull her out of gear, put the brake on and he'd go down and pick a rabbit out of a warren where he'd set a wire . . . My father used to come home with two or three rabbits in his flag basket every day of the week. So did all the gang." J. H. RUSSELL

The relationship between the tunnel and station is clearly seen in this photograph looking north on a summer afternoon. The massive structure of the over-bridge, carrying the Worcester Road across the valley of the Over Norton Brook, was a prominent feature of Chipping Norton station.

A view looking due south from the Worcester Road bridge, revealing the unmistakable setting of Chipping Norton station. J. H. MOSS

The Banbury–Kingham auto starting out from Chipping Norton on a glorious summer day in 1947. By this time the horse-chestnut trees, planted by William Bliss sixty years earlier, had reached maturity. R. WOODFIN

lar care so that the wheels of the engine didn't 'pick up' and slide on the greasy rails. Even the most skilled crews would fear not being able to bring the train to a stand at the Chipping Norton down home signal just outside the tunnel mouth.

The single track emerged from the south end of the tunnel in a cutting in a valley to the west of the town and below The Common. Here a single point connected the up and down crossing loops and, after passing beneath the substantial ' blue-brick bridge bearing the steeply-inclined Worcester Road, the two lines ran between the part-shaded curved platforms where our train came to a stand.

The setting of Chipping Norton station was truly magical, a joy to behold and incredibly difficult to describe with adequate justice. The close proximity of the tunnel, the road bridge, the curving platforms, the wooded slope from the Common, the inclined footpath approach from the Worcester Road, the main drive sloping down to the station lined with mature horse-chestnut trees, the grassy surrounds, the elegant lattice footbridge, the red-brick station buildings, the stone-coloured canopies, the little wooden signal cabin, the station gardens, the cream-coloured water tanks and the red-armed signals were all ingredients which could be found elsewhere, but at Chipping Norton the way they combined in the setting was simply unforgettable. Even on the most miserable day and in pouring rain it was an inspiring sight.

Here the workers for Bliss Mill stepped out onto the platform without any hurry whatsoever because the first train got them to Chipping Norton too early for work. The coach almost emptied until a handful of businessmen, who used the train to get them to Kingham for a connection to London, came aboard.

While all this was going on, the Chipping Norton signalman assisted the guard in unloading the last few fish boxes, a substantial number of parcels and, of course, the last bundles of newspapers. The luggage compartment was looking more empty now but there was still the travelling safe into which the previous day's takings from each station had been posted as it passed along the line. There were also a number of parcels taken on board here for Kingham.

Pulling away from the station, the line continued on the right-hand curve which had begun in the tunnel and took the line around the base of the Common to connect with the alignment of the original branch line from Chipping Norton Junction. The goods yard seen from the left-hand window largely occupied the site of the original terminus which was abandoned when the line was opened through to King's Sutton and Banbury in 1887. The handsome red-brick goods shed which dominated the revised yard was of unmistakable GWR design, but, admirable though it was, it paled against the overwhelming splendour of the Bliss Tweed Mill which rose out of the most beautiful setting on the lower slopes of the Common. There can be few people who have not been impressed or even overwhelmed with their first sight of the factory which would have been a real asset to even the grandest of towns let alone such a modest little market town as Chipping Norton.

The Mill had been served by a private siding since the opening of the railway and the gasworks just further west also had its own siding.

The line left the station on a westerly course with down grades of 1 in 220, then 1 in 113 and 1 in 95 following the gentle valley of the narrow Over Norton Brook.

The stunning Bliss Tweed Mill in its magnificent setting beside the Great Common at Chipping Norton, with the beautiful Cotswold Hills as a backdrop. Built by William Bliss in 1872 to replace the earlier 'Lower Mill' which was destroyed by fire, the unique structure, designed to be fireproof, was a visual testimony of its owner's remarkable character.

DAVID JOHNSTON

The magnificent panorama of Chipping Norton from the natural vantage point of Kingham Hill, looking east. Les Floyd, who spent many years at Kingham Hill School in the 1920s and 30s, recalled the scene. "You could see the smoke (of an approaching train) coming out behind the tunnel". He was describing the north-west portal of the tunnel, out of view in this Packer photograph. Hill Farm is in the right foreground with Cornwell railway bridge beyond it. The long approach embankments were the product of the Board of Trade's decision in the summer of 1855 to replace the original level crossing at this point with a bridge. The railway is seen curving from left to right in the centre of the view, and Bliss Tweed Mill on the left immediately beyond. The most spectacular view was that from the last house in Chipping Norton on the Churchill Road, No. 1 West End. It was here that Alfred Carter lived since the age of two. Looking after his ageing father, who spent his last years up to 1936 in the house, Alfred had an uninterrupted view of the trains. Alfred would put a chair out for his father in a corner of the back kitchen where he could see the fields towards Churchill. At midday the punctual Cardiff–Newcastle express would thread its way up the valley towards Chipping Norton where he could see it approaching under the Cornwell railway bridge. Alfred recalled his father looking at his watch and with a smile saying "She's two minutes late today". The express was rarely more than two minutes late.

F. R. PACKER

After being crossed by the controversial bridge carrying the road leading from Cornwell to Chipping Norton, the line rejoined the valley of the little stream, now called the Cornwell or Swailsford Brook, and headed south-west through the most beautiful Cotswold landscape. From the left-hand window the view was of the gentle but plain green grazing land rising towards the high ground around Chipping Norton and from the right-hand window the partly-wooded grounds of Kingham Hill Homes, now called Kingham Hill School, on the broad expanse of the valley. Distant trees and hedges patterned the slopes which provided a gentle backdrop to the rows of pollarded willows marking the course of the narrow river through the lush flood plain. The gradients still fell at 1 in 100, level and 1 in 294, barely interrupted by a furlong or so of a 1 in 440 climb, then the continuing fall of 1 in 206 and 1 in 387.

The halt at Sarsden appeared on the right as the line started to veer in that direction, its unexpected presence in such a remote setting explaining the reason for the train's progressive loss of speed, until it finally came to a halt alongside the little sleeper-built platform, equipped with a pagoda-style corrugated-iron waiting shed similar to those at Milton and Rollright halts.

In the background, not far away, the gentlest breeze frequently tickled the long slender green leaves of the stumpy willows, producing a mild shimmering effect as they reflected the warming rays of the morning sun, providing one of those wonderfully tranquil moments that linger in the mind. So, too, would the sight of the lovingly tended allotment gardens down behind the platform. Looking across towards the sun, the view from the left-hand windows overlooked the small goods yard where a single open wagon stood on the adjacent siding, overlooked by a little blue-brick signal box of unmistakable GWR origin. It was hard to imagine a Newcastle to Cardiff express passing through this lost backwater.

As the train pulled away from this idyllic spot, it ran across the narrow lane by means of the first gated crossing encountered on this journey, yet just one third of a mile further on was another where the line ran over a minor road connecting the villages of Kingham and Churchill.

From Sarsden the line gently meandered along the valley with down grades of 1 in 98 and 1 in 207 interrupted by a quarter-mile climb at 1 in 219, then down grades of 1 in 644, 1 in 206, level, 1 in 107, and 1 in 194 to Kingham.

Viewed from the opposite side of the valley to the previous photograph but towards the west. The beautiful Cotswolds stretch away towards Stow-on-the-Wold, in the far right distance. The Cornwell Brook with its rows of willows flows from right to left. The railway passed close by, with the ground frame shelter at the north-east end of the loop siding featuring in the centre foreground. c.1930.
CHIPPING NORTON MUSEUM

General view of Sarsden Halt, looking due north. The willows bordering the brook are visible behind the platform. Former Banbury engineman Stan Cowley recalls "Mrs. Grizzell got on at Sarsden – she was in the railway police – nobody knew a lot about her."
LENS OF SUTTON

CHURCHILL THE COTSWOLDS FROM

The railway in the landscape. The glorious Cotswold panorama, looking due west over Churchill Mill and Sarsden Halt, c.1930 with stooks in the fields and thatched haystacks of a vanished era. The village of Kingham is seen in the left distance, with Churchill Crossing centre left and the white post of the tall Kingham East distant signal to the left of the crossing. CHIPPING NORTON MUSEUM

The final stretch of the journey to Kingham begins at Churchill Crossing, just off the left-hand edge of this photograph looking due east. The railway is seen running from left to right on a shallow embankment across the centre of this view, which also shows the Kingham Road ascending the hill into Churchill. The 19th-century village church, prominent on the horizon, was built to replace an earlier structure located behind the trees to the left of the road. The present church tower was modelled on that of Magdalen College, Oxford. The three sons of Churchill crossing keeper Arthur Watkins and his wife Alice, lived with Arthur's mother in one of the houses in the Kingham Road (in the centre of view) to ease the cramped conditions of the crossing lodge.

COLLECTION ALAN WATKINS

Shortly before passing beneath a bridge carrying the road which connects the village of Kingham to the B4450 Stow to Chipping Norton road, the single line divided into the up and down lines of the double track which led towards Kingham station. The bridge, known as New Line Bridge, was so named in 1855 to differentiate it from the one spanning the Oxford to Worcester line at the newly-built junction. Careful observers may have noticed the original stonework facing the northern abutment which had been retained in the 1906 rebuilding.

Kingham East signal box stood on the left immediately beyond the bridge, adjacent to a double junction connecting with the 1906 loop line which, forking slightly to the right, led onto an embankment over the OWWR main line to provide direct connection to the western portion of the Banbury & Cheltenham Direct.

Kingham East Junction, where the 1906 Direct loop diverged to the right and the branch curved southwards towards Kingham station to the left. This 1950s picture was taken from the 'New Line Bridge'. George Edwards and Ern Hartley were the two regular signalmen at Kingham East for many years. In the postwar years, when this photograph was taken, Harold Hall relieved for one of the signalmen, and took the opportunity of cleaning up the cabin, which had been neglected during the war years. When the signalmen returned, the lino floor was so shiny that the signalmen (who were both tall men) kept slipping on the surface. The problem was solved by them shovelling soot from the stove onto the floor!
J. H. MOSS

The double-track curve on the right brought trains from Banbury and Chipping Norton into the branch platforms alongside the OWWR main line. 6th October 1951.
P. J. GARLAND

Looking north from the station footbridge, with the Cheltenham platform on the left and the Banbury arrival platform on the right. 6th October 1951.
P. J. GARLAND

No. 1473 with the 'Kingham Car' alongside the Banbury arrival platform on 18th September 1948. The engine was being watered prior to working the return journey.
R. E. TUSTIN

The Kingham auto was routed on the down line towards Kingham station, the double-track approach to which curved sharply southwards through 90 degrees in order to arrive parallel to the alignment of the main line. The gentle meandering passage through the dreamy landscape was suddenly brought to an end with the sound of the wheels clattering over the pointwork, then squealing around the curve past the engine shed and water tower. The sight of the impressive mainline junction station with all its signals, various buildings and canopies, contrasted sharply to the quiet establishments along the branch. Here trains from both Banbury and Cheltenham were accommodated at a pair of platforms to the east of the main-line ones.

When the passengers who had boarded at Chipping Norton alighted to make their way over the footbridge to the up main platform to catch the London train, the single autocar suddenly felt strangely deserted. The journey, the combination of people making use of the train, the angle of the sun over the landscape and the way it had played on the interior as the coach had changed axis along the meandering route, had now all passed – only the smell of fish lingered in the metal tray in the luggage van.

Having completed his first trip of the day, the Banbury driver who had stopped the engine "right for water", pulled the long arm of the water crane across the platform and handed the chain to the fireman who had climbed up on top of the tanks and opened the lids ready to put the leather 'bag' in to refill them for the return journey.

And there we leave this description of the line. For reasons of space, Kingham station and the route to Cheltenham are covered in the third volume of this work.

Old Oak Common-based No. 6003 King George IV *tearing through King's Sutton station with the 7.40 a.m. Birkenhead–Paddington on 8th September 1962. Before the provision of the footbridge c.1909, the boarded crossing was the only means of access to the down platform. Thereafter it was only used by the staff to take parcels and milk churns over the line. King's Sutton station first opened in 1872. GWR Board minutes for 18th October 1871 record the acceptance of a tender for station and buildings at King's Sutton for £1,648. The following month they record 'the contract for the station provides for a larger station building with longer platforms than had been first estimated and consequently a further £603, making a total of £2,916 is necessary. The approach and goods yard will be constructed by Co's staff.' The physical appearance of the station is a mystery. Following inspection of the completed works, the Board of Trade officer Colonel Yolland's report simply refers to 'the erection of a passenger station with platforms and shelter', whilst the 1873 deposited plans for the Banbury & Cheltenham Direct Railway show only one building approximately 22ft long by 7ft wide. The next reference, the GWR Board minutes for 2nd January 1884, record that the B&C Co 'had paid the sum of £4,000, the amount they would have had to expend at King's Sutton Junction if the traffic were exchanged there, this company [the GWR] being at liberty to expend the money upon works there or at Banbury, as they may think proper, constructing in the latter event at King's Sutton an ordinary double junction estimated to cost £730 . . .' At the same meeting, expenditure of £3,730 was authorised 'for works at King's Sutton and Banbury in addition to the £4,000 from the Banbury and Cheltenham.' Plans accompanying the BoT report for the inspection of the B&C between King's Sutton and Chipping Norton in 1884 clearly show the approximately 50ft x 20ft building seen on the opposite page, but whether, as seems likely, it was a replacement for an earlier smaller structure is not clear. The total £7,730 available for works in connection with the exchange of traffic at King's Sutton and Banbury could well have included the new buildings and down side waiting shelter.*

R. A. F. PURYER

CHAPTER NINE

THE STATIONS

KING'S SUTTON

82m 55c

No. 6903 on the 11.5 a.m. (SO) Wolverhampton to Weymouth train passing King's Sutton on 4th August 1962. If the station building was an 1884 replacement of an earlier one, this would tie in well with the fact that the design was repeated at Adderbury, Bloxham and Hook Norton, and the absence of any other examples of this design elsewhere on the GWR would support such a supposition. MICHAEL HALE

IN the 1920s the station master at King's Sutton was Harry Gardner who had held the position there since 1910. He supervised the station and also the ironstone workings at Astrop, between Banbury and King's Sutton.

By the mid-1920s railway staff directly supervised by the King's Sutton station master were six signalmen (three at Astrop and three at King's Sutton); a signal porter based at King's Sutton, but allocated to Sydenham signal box to release ironstone trains from the siding there; one porter and lad porter; two clerks, one of whom was the station master's son; two permanent way gangs, King's Sutton and Aynho; and in addition two pumpers to control the Nell Bridge troughs, a signal linesman and a telegraph linesman – a total of 27 staff.

John Fortnum joined the Great Western as a lad porter at King's Sutton in 1927. He had left school at the age of 14 but as he could not enter service with the railway until he was 16, he spent two years as an errand boy for the Banbury wholesale firm of Brummitts.

John recalls the station staff in 1927 were as follows:

STATION STAFF
Harry Gardner – station master
Tom Gardner – clerk
Jimmy Neville – clerk
Sam Berry – signal porter
Harry Croft – porter
John Fortnum – lad porter
Billy Hall – signalman
Frank Calcutt – signalman
Bill Pratt – signalman

PERMANENT WAY STAFF
King's Sutton Gang Astrop to Nell Bridge
Albert Adkins – ganger
Herbert Atkins – sub-ganger
George Mobley
(Aubrey) George Fortnum
Harry Green
Bill Hall
Ivor Proberts
Jack Rymell

Aynho Gang
Bill Troth – ganger
Harry Hickman
Bert Bint
? Cox
Bert Dunn
Benny Hawkins

Pumpers (for Nell Bridge Troughs)
Arthur Owen
? Proberts

Astrop Signalmen
Len Cadd
Harold Bowne (replaced Jimmy West c.1928)
Frank Geare

John Fortnum started work at 8.0 a.m. and walked to the station from his parents' home in the village. The early-turn porter had already unlocked the station gates, but occasionally he overslept, and so John, who was issued with the spare set of keys, would be called out to unlock them.

The lad porter's duty was 8.0 a.m. until 5.0 p.m. with an hour for lunch. The two adult porters swapped early and late turns from 5.45 a.m. to 1.45 p.m. with an hour for lunch, and 1.30 p.m. to 10.30 p.m. with an hour for tea. The lad porter would be required to book passenger tickets, meet the trains, open and close carriage doors, help with passengers' luggage and take tickets. This last job was really an adult porter's job, but if Harry Gardner, the station master, was there, John was allowed to do it. Upon arrival of passenger trains, the porters would call out "King's Sutton, change here for Bicester, Oxford and all stations to Kingham."

John helped in the booking office, sorting the tickets alphabetically and numerically, ready to be sent to the Audit Office in London. Blank cards were tied up separately and put in a parcel with the others.

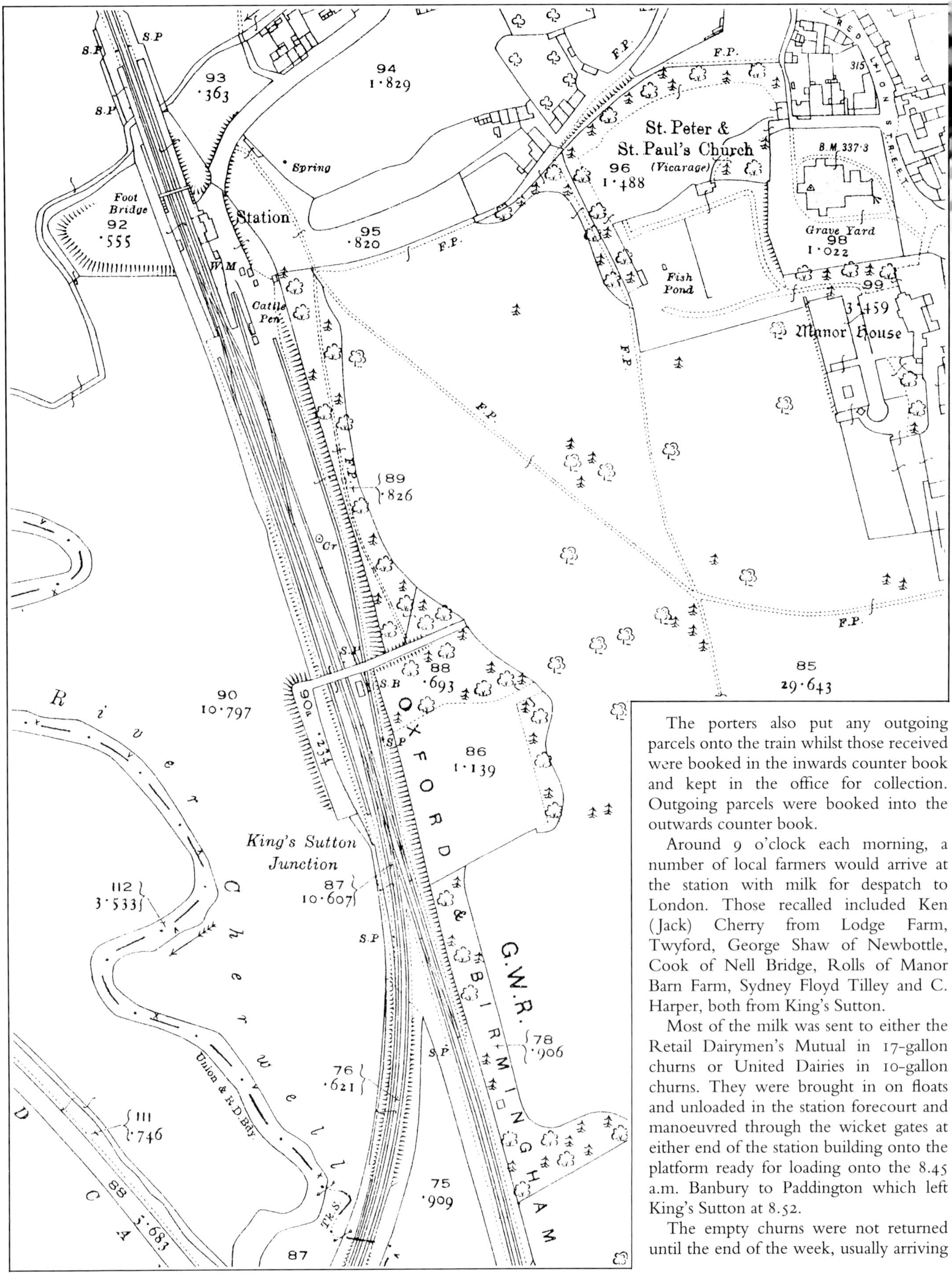

Taken from 25-inch OS map for 1922.

The porters also put any outgoing parcels onto the train whilst those received were booked in the inwards counter book and kept in the office for collection. Outgoing parcels were booked into the outwards counter book.

Around 9 o'clock each morning, a number of local farmers would arrive at the station with milk for despatch to London. Those recalled included Ken (Jack) Cherry from Lodge Farm, Twyford, George Shaw of Newbottle, Cook of Nell Bridge, Rolls of Manor Barn Farm, Sydney Floyd Tilley and C. Harper, both from King's Sutton.

Most of the milk was sent to either the Retail Dairymen's Mutual in 17-gallon churns or United Dairies in 10-gallon churns. They were brought in on floats and unloaded in the station forecourt and manoeuvred through the wicket gates at either end of the station building onto the platform ready for loading onto the 8.45 a.m. Banbury to Paddington which left King's Sutton at 8.52.

The empty churns were not returned until the end of the week, usually arriving on various trains, often at night, over the weekend. On Monday mornings, the staff would arrive to find the down platform full of empty churns, which the porters barrowed over the crossings at the end of the platforms and put into the forecourt ready for the farmers to collect.

King's Sutton goods yard was serviced by 'the Bletchington', a pick-up goods which worked through from Banbury to Bletchington on the Banbury–Oxford line. It called at King's Sutton at 9.15 a.m., then all intermediate stations and was worked back by a change-over crew on a late shift.

The pick-up invariably included a 'roadside' van which originated from Hockley. When the train was formed at Banbury, the van was positioned immediately in front of the brake van. Roadside traffic was known as 'smalls' and typically consisted of perishables such as flour, oil or sacks of corn. Traffic for King's Sutton was transferred into the lock-up goods shed on the platform to be dealt with by the porters and clerical staff.

All roadside goods received were signed for on arrival. Ideally, items would arrive with the top copy of an invoice originating from the sending station. The invoice would be taken into the booking office and entered into the goods received book, which the consignee would sign on collection.

From time to time, goods traffic arrived without an invoice, and in this situation the clerks entered the details in the 'unentered' book, and contacted the sending station for a copy of the invoice to be sent forward.

Roadside traffic occasionally originated from King's Sutton. John Fortnum recalled sacks of potatoes being sent by his father, George, to his uncle, Bert Godfrey, in Herne Bay.

John took his lunch break from 12.30 to 1.30 and he usually went home. The porters and lad porters were always required to be flexible in their approach, moving from one task to another requiring immediate attention; priority would be given to a large goods consignment, for example.

One of the seasonal arrivals were racing pigeons which were sent to King's Sutton and countless other stations throughout the country for release. "We used to get

The bottom end of Wales Street became known as Station Road and it entered the Station Yard through a wooden gate which was locked at night. The station building was flanked either side by two gates and it was here that the milk churns were stored. Next to the northernmost gate was a wooden hut, which housed the station gas meter. The main station building was entered through a pair of doors, which opened directly into the general waiting room. The doors were slightly right of centre of the room, so that to the left, behind the door, was a row of fixed benches, mirrored on the inside of the doors leading onto the platform, so the benches faced each other. The only furniture was a sturdy wooden table in the centre of the room, the right-hand wall featuring a hearth and mantelshelf and the left-hand wall a door giving access to the booking office, to the right of which was the ticket window. In one of the two corners nearest the platform was a Nestlés chocolate machine. The booking office, a large room occupying the full width of the building, was the hub of the station's activities and was equipped for the necessary clerical duties. The wall facing the approach road was plain, broken only by a window overlooking the yard area. On a string was hung a bunch of consignment notes for goods and parcels traffic and on the floor was a paste pot for affixing labels to parcels. As the long south-facing external gable wall was windowless, it provided ample room for a set of spring-balanced scales. Alongside this was the ticket storage cupboard, a fireplace, a rack containing the general appendices, rates and reference manuals. In the corner nearest the platform was a wall-mounted local exchange telephone equipped with two buttons which enabled it to be switched between the local exchange and the stations and signal boxes in the district. In front of the rack containing the appendices was the station master's desk and on this was a telephone connected to the national exchange, including Banbury. The opposite wall to the desk featured a full-length counter, interrupted only by the door to the waiting room. Centrally positioned in this was the ticket window, flanked to the left by a ticket rack containing hundreds of pre-printed tickets. This rack was formed in three sections, with the racks built into doors which folded away neatly when not in use. On the right was the ticket press. Under the window was the office safe. The nearer of the two doors in the northern gable wall led into the porter's room and was mainly used for stowing bicycles for the day return passengers to Oxford. The other one led into the gents' lavatory, containing a urinal, separate water closet and washbasin. The cubicle was entered by putting a penny in the slot and it was the porter's duty to periodically empty it out. This was done by picking the lock with a length of bent wire, kept for the purpose. A row of fire buckets for use in case of emergency was prominently positioned in the fence facing the Gents.

J. H. MOSS

Looking south from the down platform c.1962. LENS OF SUTTON

the baskets out of the vans and line them all up on the platform and release them." Afterwards the porters emptied out the chippings and sent the baskets back to the sender.

One of the essential porter's duties was refuelling the signal lamps and the lad porter usually carried this out. Three days a week were given to lamping – one each for King's Sutton, Astrop and Sydenham. The fuel drums were kept in a lock-up hut next to the station weighbridge and the porter was required to travel out to all signals on foot to refuel the lamps.

The Astrop signals were some distance from King's Sutton and John Fortnum used to cycle rather than walk (quite unofficially!) out to the Astrop up distant signal at Franklin's Knob, some three miles from King's Sutton.

Other duties included sweeping platforms and pumping water to fill the lavatory cisterns. It took about a hundred pumping actions per day to fill the tanks – even more at weekends when the station was busier. The porter knew when the tank was full because the overflow would discharge into the urinal. The last duty of the day was to take a bucketful of water and sluice down the Gents' urinal.

The senior porter on the late shift was responsible for closing and locking the station gates when he booked off duty at 10.30 p.m.

At one time King's Sutton station had gardens for which the village was renowned, a rose garden extending from the main station building towards the goods shed, a rock garden reaching towards the southern platform ramp and a second rock garden at the southern end of the down platform. Throughout the second two decades of the twentieth century, the station garden was meticulously maintained by the station master, Harry Gardner, who won the divisional competition every year he entered. Although he took full responsibility for the care of the station gardens, the staff could be called upon to assist if the need arose. No detail was overlooked; if the edges of the platform slabs needed weeding, the porters used the hooked end of a shunting pole to dislodge the earth. Harry Gardner would share out a proportion of the prize money among his staff in recognition of their contribution. The story has been told that when he pruned the rose heads, he stamped on the trimmings so that nobody could graft from the cuttings. In the effort to upkeep such a high standard, the station master must surely have trodden a fine line between professional excellence and obsessive endeavour. One woman recalled how, as a young girl, she accidentally stepped from the platform onto the border, for which the station master reprimanded her with a slap across the face. The girl went on to become the deputy headmistresses of the village school. H. J. STRETTON WARD

The last years of the decade were very insecure for railway workers due to the slump arising from the Wall Street crash. At King's Sutton the two clerks' positions were axed in line with similar cutbacks elsewhere. The clerical duties were divided amongst the porters.

Had it not been for the economies of the time, John would have been promoted to an adult porter's position at the age of 19 but instead he faced redundancy. However, as John was a valued member of the station staff, station master Harry Gardner wrote to the District Superintendent, 'Big White Chief' Bill Barnes at Birmingham, and asked him if John could stay at King's Sutton as a porter if he was willing to remain on the junior porter's rate of thirty-five shillings a week. This was agreed.

At the close of the decade, the age of entering service on the GWR was lowered from sixteen to fourteen and the first of these recruits at King's Sutton was Jimmy Russell who, many years later, went on to write a number of railway books including *The Banbury & Cheltenham Railway* published by OPC.

Jim left King's Sutton and joined the Royal Engineers in 1934, being a

Leaving the general waiting room through the double door, the passengers arrived on the platform under a large canopy. Turning to their right, a single door gave access to the ladies' waiting room and lavatory. Flowing through a culvert beneath the platforms was a foul-smelling water course known as Black Brook. The railway was carried over the brook by means of a steel girder bridge, the platform sides actually forming the curved segmental arch for this passage. The water from this stream supplied the station gardens and was drawn out in the fire buckets which the porters lowered into the water. The corrugated-iron shed was used for the storage of goods received from the roadside van. There was a Pooley weighing machine inside. P. J. GARLAND

CLERICAL DUTIES

In addition to a daily record of ticket sales logged in what was known as the 'booking up book' or 'booking clerks train book', there were weekly summaries or 'proofs'. At King's Sutton these were carried out on Fridays. It was necessary to ensure ticket sales agreed with the last number of each type of ticket left unsold. Each rack of tickets therefore had a small slate which was used to chalk on the next ticket number. This visual record was maintained by the clerk as a means of cross-checking the various ticket issues in the daily and weekly records. In many cases there were no printed tickets for children so adult tickets were converted for use by being cut in half – diagonally in the case of returns and squarely for singles. If it was not possible to halve the fare exactly, the clerk charged the larger amount and extra was recorded in the surplus book.

As John Fortnum explains – "a single ticket to Banbury cost 5½d. The clerks had to charge 3d for a half ticket to the passenger. If the second half was subsequently issued, we also had to charge 3d so another ½d went into the surplus cash book."

If there was no printed ticket for a destination, a blank card was issued which, in the case of a half fare ticket, had to be overstamped 'child'. Any of the half tickets still left in the racks were removed at the end of each month and the slate altered. "If, for example, the tickets amounted to say 183½d, we made our records out to 184. We sent them on to the Audit Office, taking a credit of a ½d on the return."

Also at the end of the month, the clerks prepared the accounts for audit, John Fortnum recalling, "There were hundreds of them", all broken down into different railway companies and sections of railways. Great Western allocations were called locals and all others were called RCH (Railway Clearing House). The Great Western and Great Central Joint Railway accounts, for example, went through the Railway Clearing House. Passengers' classification had to be forwarded by the third day of each month. Parcels had to go on the 5th day and goods on the 8th day.

For the booking of milk traffic, farmers gave a consignment note to the station master. The clerks booked it into a long format 'accounts paid' ledger, entered daily, and John remembered going round and collecting money once a month from those who had to be chased for late payment.

A float of £2 was retained and the balance was sent on to the GWR company accountant in a cash bag kept locked in a safe in the brake van on the 7.24. A stamped 'return by train' form accompanied it, in an accountancy envelope. A tear-off portion was returned and filed.

The cash for staff wages arrived every Thursday afternoon, the bag being conveyed by a relief station master who travelled in a locked first class compartment on the 3.25 Banbury to Oxford train.

The station master and clerks, although on a monthly salaried paybill of thirteen 4-weekly periods, received an interim payment every second Thursday. On the fourth Thursday, the balance of their monthly salary was paid less stoppages.

Uniformed staff were paid each Thursday in order of seniority, i.e. the junction signalmen, the Astrop signalmen, porter signalman Sam Berry and finally porter Harry Croft.

The first task was to count the cash and reconcile it with the paybills. Then John Fortnum and the station master would "do the money up", both counted it and put it in tobacco tins labelled with the staff member's name. When the staff came in to collect their wages, the station master countersigned the paybill and this was always witnessed.

The paybills were then returned to Wolverhampton. Wages not claimed were locked in the safe and a note was entered into the unpaid wages book which the recipient signed when collected.

A separate paybill was made out to Paid Widows and Orphans and sick pay through Provident Mutual.

Staff not covered by the King's Sutton paybill were those representing the two permanent way gangs, who were covered by Wolverhampton, and the Nell Bridge trough pumpers, the signal linesman and the telegraph linesman, whose paybills were made out through the Engineering Department at Tyseley. The station master was on a salaried paybill.

Supplementary Reservist with the GWR, and went on to become a guard based at Banbury. He spent much of his working life on the Banbury & Cheltenham Railway and later, when he left the railway about 1947 to start a photography business in Banbury, he went on to take some of the most valuable photographs used in this book.

In the early 1930s, Sam Berry, the signal-porter, retired and John Fortnum replaced him as Grade 2 porter. His wages, previously frozen at thirty-five shillings per week, went up to two pounds.

Porters came and went with great regularity. Harry Croft was replaced by Bert Claridge, who arrived in the early 1930s and left the railway to set up a fruiterer's business in Coventry. He was then replaced by Reg Lynes who moved up from junior porter. It was around 1932–3 that station master Harry Gardner retired. He continued living at his home in Astrop Gardens and the post was temporarily filled by a relief station master Harris, until Leonard Almond arrived.

STAFF c.1932–3

Leonard Almond – station master
John Fortnum – grade 2 porter
Reg Lynes – porter
Harry Calcutt – lad porter
Frank Calcutt – signalman
Bert Wright – signalman

Leo Almond, known as 'Nutty' to railway staff, lived opposite the new school in Richmond Street. He had three daughters, one of whom eventually became clerk to him at King's Sutton. He was a keen fisherman, who also engaged

This view of a single-coach train heading south for Bicester provides a good idea of the station's surroundings with the impressive screen of horse-chestnut trees along the eastern boundary and the water meadows to the right. The Banbury & Cheltenham line can just be made out curving away to the right beyond the bridge carrying a farm track over the line. The goods yard, occupied by a handful of coal wagons, had been equipped with a 2-ton fixed hand crane which had stood at the south end adjacent to the siding nearest to the running lines. The siding serving the cattle pens on the dock behind the up platform could hold up to three cattle wagons. The siding on the right once served as an up refuge. The down platform waiting shelter contained a chocolate bar vending machine which the porters periodically raided when the booking office was short of petty cash! P. J. GARLAND

Set back across the yard adjacent to the station boundary was the Pooley cart weighbridge and office. The corrugated-iron shed alongside was for the storage of signal lamp oil, whilst barely apparent behind this was the Signal and Telegraph linesman's hut. Just below, between the S&T hut and the spinney, was the permanent way hut.
P. J. GARLAND

GOODS TRAFFIC

OUTWARDS

Hay – Hay cut in late spring was usually transported in the autumn. John Fortnum recalls Harry Tustian of Milton bringing it to the station for despatch to Griffiths, a merchant in South Lambeth, who purchased a whole rick to supply feed for railway horses. As the consignor paid by the wagon, it was in his interest to ensure it was fully loaded. "Tustian gave me many a ten-shilling note to make sure I got a full load on."

The technique for loading the trusses was exacting. "We filled the bed up with trusses on end and then laid the next layer transversely and so on, gradually bringing the level up so that it was finished with one truss up the middle. The loaded wagons were covered with two sheets of tarpaulin, lapped to take account of the direction of travel so that the wind could not get under it. Two ropes were tied buffer to buffer and across the sides and then it was passed under the loading gauge."

The empty wagons arrived on the pickup goods service and the King's Sutton staff always ordered the LMS 12-ton common user, because it was the only wagon big enough to hold a full load.

Sugar beet – In the autumn season during the 1920s, sugar beet was harvested from local farms and loaded into wagons at King's Sutton. This annual consignment was not charged to the farmers, as carriage costs were borne by the Government. The farm labourers were responsible for loading up the wagons.

Timber – Regular supplies of round timber were brought to the station for despatch, but as the weight was beyond the capacity of the 2-ton yard crane, on each occasion a travelling crane was ordered especially for the purpose from Worcester.

Livestock – The proximity of Banbury's cattle market meant that quite large numbers of cattle were handled at the station, chiefly on Thursdays, which was market day. They were transported in specially ordered cattle wagons.

Sir Mervyn Manningham Buller of Charlton would often send his prize bulls from King's Sutton to various shows around the country. They travelled in special vehicles which the GWR code-named 'BEETLES'.

The Bicester Hunt was a not uncommon visitor to King's Sutton and the horses were transported there in horseboxes code-named 'PACOs'. On arrival these were shunted across the spur next to the crane and pushed manually into the dock with a pinchbar. As the dock was only long enough to accommodate three vehicles at a time, after unloading, the empties were pushed into the back road to allow the next ones to reach the dock. This was a lengthy and very demanding operation for the porters, but if there was a sufficient number of horse-boxes, an engine was sent out from Banbury to shunt them.

Once the PACOs were in the back road, it was the porters' job to 'rough clean' them. This was not a pleasant task. After the manure had been shovelled out for use on the station gardens, the wagons were scrubbed out with a wire brush and No. 2 disinfectant. (No. 1 disinfectant was used for the station lavatories.) The wagons were then sent on to Banbury for cleansing.

Owen Judd's delivery lorry outside King's Sutton post office c.1932. The figure on the left was Burt Humphries, driver, followed by Geoffrey Judd (Owen's son) and Owen Judd.
CTY. GEOFFREY JUDD

No. 5922 Caxton Hall, *from Oxford shed, approaching King's Sutton station with the 1.32 p.m. Portsmouth Harbour–Birmingham (Snow Hill), composed of LMS-design stock. 8th September 1962.* R. A. F. PURYER

INWARDS

Coal – In common with so many other stations, coal was the main incoming traffic at King's Sutton station. Owen Judd, the local coal merchant, held wharfage at the station and supplied local users including the village merchant, Jack Bint.

Judd had a named wagon which was conveyed in the daily pick-up goods. His supplies came from three collieries, Baddesley, Cannock and Littleton.

In the 1920s Owen Judd's driver was Bill Humphries. Before delivering coal, the motor lorry and its load was weighed on the cart weighbridge by the station porters and charged to the merchant according to a measured scale.

Incidentally, the coal merchant was allowed two clear days to empty his wagon before incurring a sidings rent charge of 6d per day. Ordinary common users failing to clear their wagons in the two-day period were charged demurrage at the more expensive rate of 3s. 6d.

MISCELLANEOUS TRAFFIC

One memorable occasional consignment was rejected flour and wheat grain, which was purchased by Stephen Spokes of Hollands Farm, from the railway salvage department at Shoreditch, London, for use as pig feed. It was transported in a motor lorry and after emptying, the wagons were despatched to Tyseley to be disinfected.

CARRIERS

William Barbour was a local carrier whose business was based at his home in Newbottle Road (colloquially known as Barbour's Hill after him). In 1927 his son, George, began helping and eventually took over the business. Almost every night he would arrive at the station with his horse and cart to see if there was any 'Paid Home' traffic. Very often there was and whichever member of staff was available would pay William Barbour the agreed cost of carriage, and recharge it to the sending station on a way bill. The clerk would collect the necessary payment from the consignor.

'2301' class 0–6–0 No. 2406 easing out of the yard at King's Sutton with what was probably the 9.35 a.m. Oxford to Bordesley pick-up on a bright winter's day c.1922. The train, which was due into King's Sutton at 12.25 p.m., was the only down local goods to serve King's Sutton at this time, and was scheduled to spent half an hour in the yard. By 1925, the 6.46 p.m. Kingham to Banbury pick-up was also scheduled to make a call when required, just after 11.0 p.m., but this arrangement did not survive for long. L&GRP

Another local carrier was Charlie Frost, who came from the nearby village of Charlton. He was an epileptic who knew when the onset of a seizure was about to occur. As John Fortnum recalled, "He would stop the horse, get down off the side of the van, lay down in the verge until the seizure had passed, then get back into the cart and off he would go."

King's Sutton station supplied its own ropes and if the hay was designated for a foreign company's station, "we had to raise a charge of 15 shillings per rope and entered 'Paid on Carriage and to Pay' on the invoice which ensured that the ropes came back to King's Sutton via the same route."

No. 3809 from Banbury shed coming off the Banbury & Cheltenham onto the down main line at King's Sutton with a train of vans on 8th September 1962. R. A. F. PURYER

in a bit of shooting, and was a member of the lay preaching circuit at the Baptist chapel in Wales Street.

During his time at King's Sutton, John Fortnum's family moved from Astrop Gardens to Station Road, first to No. 5 and then to No. 3.

The proximity to the station was important because John's father, George, was the Call Man, whose job it was to call out the permanent way staff he needed during foggy weather or to clear points in heavy snow.

If there was a snowfall or heavy frost, then the signalman would call George to thaw out the points at the junction ready for the first train up the Kingham line at 6.30 a.m. This was done with a special salt formulation. King's Sutton signal box was normally closed on Sundays, although the signalman would book on if there was a Sunday excursion over the Banbury & Cheltenham. On Mondays the signalman opened the box at 6.0 a.m.

John's posting at King's Sutton ended c.1934 when he topped the signalling class examinations and was posted to Tackley as a temporary summer relief signalman, before going on to the Banbury 'Hump' Yard.

The immaculate interior of the signal box, seen in the early 1960s. S. BOLAN

No. 6022 King Edward III *from Wolverhampton Stafford Road approaching King's Sutton at speed with the 1.10 p.m. Paddington–Chester–Birkenhead on 8th September 1962.* R. A. F. PURYER

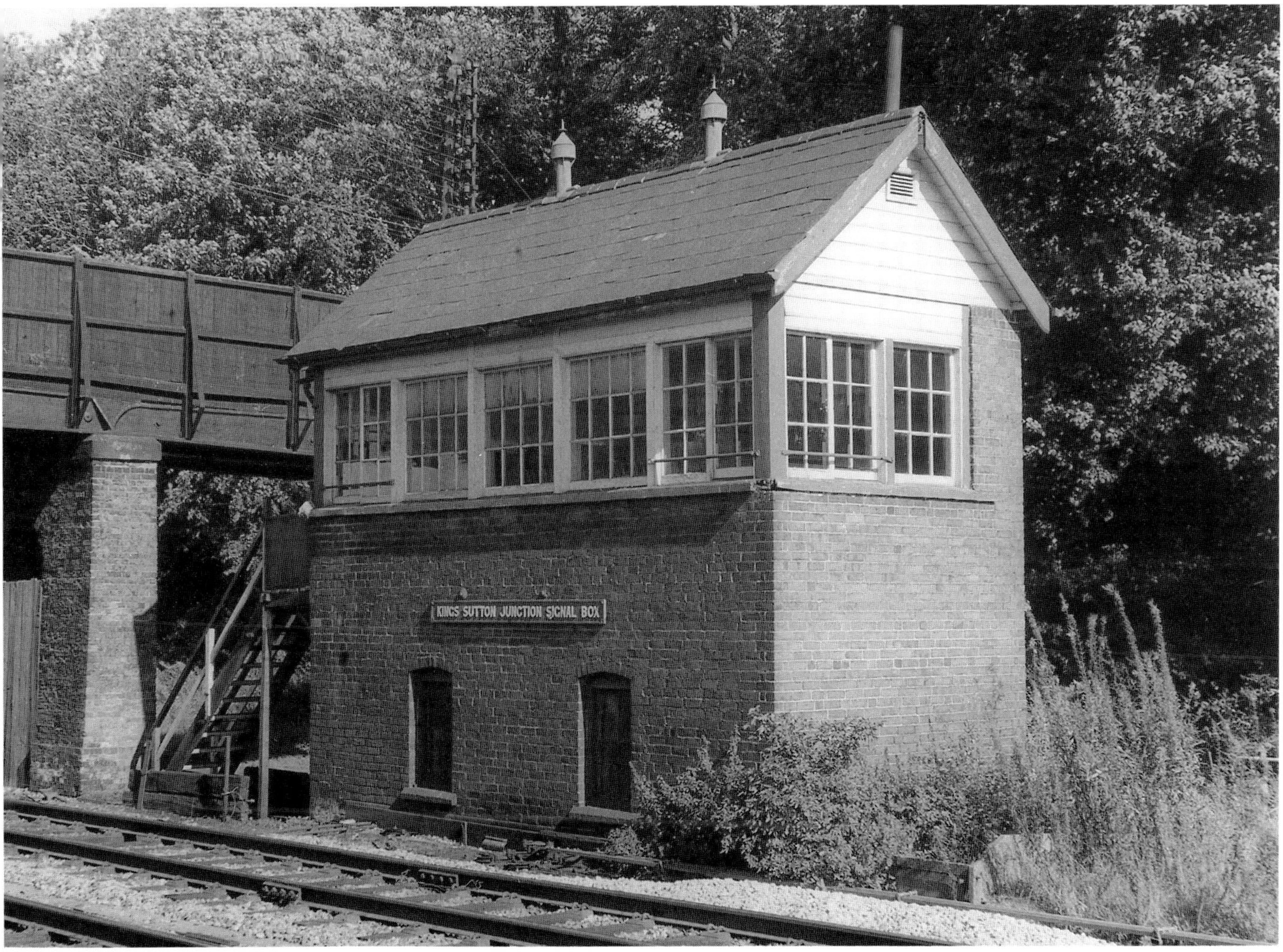

The signal box, built by McKenzie & Holland in 1884, had contained a 33-lever frame, but a replacement vertical-tappet 3-bar frame with 37 levers was installed and brought into use on 7th February 1911. There is a strong tradition of keeping signal box interiors impressively clean and at King's Sutton in the 1920s, signalman Bill Hall used to black-lead the lever frame and the stove with Zeebo, whilst Bill Pratt was responsible for polishing the brasses and Frank Calcutt cleaned the windows. They all took turns to wash the lino floor. A. W. DONALDSON

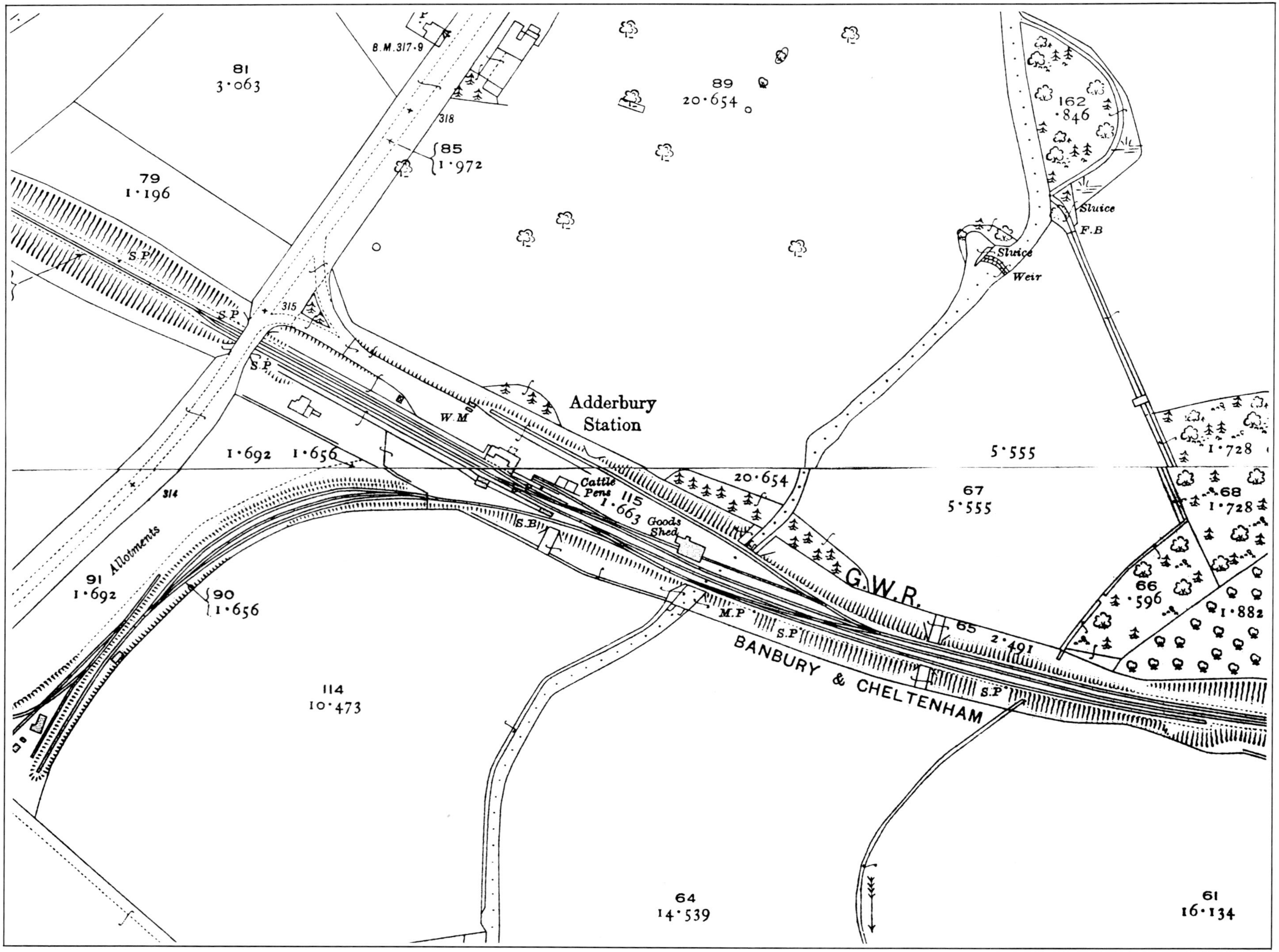

Adderbury
Station
G.W.R.
BANBURY & CHELTENHAM
Goods
Shed
Cattle
Pens
S.B.
M.P.
S.P.
W.M.
Sluice
F.B.
Weir
Allotments
B.M. 317·9
318
315
314
81
3·063
79
1·196
85
1·972
89
20·654
162
·846
5·555
67
5·555
1·728
68
1·728
66
·596
1·882
65
2·491
115
1·663
1·692
1·656
91
1·692
90
1·656
114
10·473
64
14·539
61
16·134

ADDERBURY 84m 8c

Looking east over Adderbury station from the A423 road bridge, with a Banbury–Kingham autotrain approaching and the signalman on the down platform about to hand the single-line token for the section ahead to the fireman, c.1951. R. H. G. SIMPSON

According to official records, the number of passengers purchasing tickets at Adderbury during the 1930s was meagre, averaging between 12 and 18 per week, outgoing parcels amounted to 3–4 per week whilst outgoing goods merchandise averaged just 4–7 tons per week. Even 'other minerals', which presumably referred to ironstone, ranged from an average of less than 1 ton to, say, 15 tons per week, with the exception of 1937 when a total of 2,638 tons was recorded. The figures for incoming traffic were slightly better, with weekly averages of 24–32 parcels, 44–60 tons of coal, 3–7 tons of other minerals (lime and perhaps roadstone?), 4–8 tons general merchandise.

We haven't managed to trace any surviving station staff from Adderbury but, judging from the figures, it must have been a very quiet station at this time. Indeed, the recollection of laundry girl Emily Neville, returning home to Bloxham as one of the few passengers to use the last train of the day, underlines the point.

Villagers travelling in and out of Banbury may have preferred to use the daily motor omnibus service offered by Richard A. Plackett who had run a carrier service to the Coach & Horses in Banbury since at least 1911. The motor bus, which had run since 1924, was driven by Richard's son Arthur. According to one villager, the business was run by Arthur in partnership with Willmotts. In 1930 the buses ran every half hour to Banbury and fares were 4d for a single and 6d return. The service was taken over by Trinders in the 1930s.

The principal source of traffic at Adderbury was the private siding to the south of the station, originally provided for the Hook Norton Ironstone Partnership in 1890. Ore was shipped from the quarry by narrow gauge railway. The details of the iron ore workings along the line will be dealt with in Volume Three but, to summarise here: after the HNIP went into liquidation in 1903, ownership of the workings and private siding passed to Cochrane & Co. of Dudley who opened new pits, then closed in 1922 during the postwar slump. From 1925, T. Cashmore carried out quarrying operations and from 1928 Duffield Iron Corporation took over, experimenting with a patent method of iron ore reduction, and closed in 1939.

The premises had a completely unexpected new lease of life when they were taken over by the Ministry of Aircraft Production to house a branch of the Northern Aluminium Company which was based at Southam Road, Banbury. In May 1941, the GWR authorised £620 for 'reconditioning Duffield Iron Corporation's siding... cost of work to be borne by the Ministry of Aircraft Production'.

The new factory, established adjacent to Adderbury station, shadowed the factory in Southam Road and even became known as the 'Shadow Factory'. Converting the buildings was rapid and it became a centre for reprocessing metal from

The eastern approach to Adderbury station during the final years with the goods yard on the right, down refuge on the left and premises of Twyford Seeds in the left background.
A. W. DONALDSON

TWYFORD SEEDS

Twyford Seeds Ltd. was established at Twyford Mill, King's Sutton in 1936 by local farmer Ken Cherry and William Watkinson, a gentleman of St. Mary's Mount, Worcester Road, Great Malvern. The two men saw the potential for an animal feed mixing and distribution centre to serve areas of Northamptonshire, Oxfordshire and Warwickshire. In April 1946 the premises at Twyford were destroyed in a fire so the company moved to Adderbury and took over the by then redundant premises of the Northern Aluminium Co. where a seed handling plant was installed ready for the autumn trade that year.

Although at the time of the move, Cherry and Watkinson still owned the company, they had also joined forces with a Peter Hoskins who became general manager and was largely responsible for expansion.

The company dealt primarily in animal feed and seeds. The feed was purchased from suppliers such as Bibbys, Spillers, etc. whilst seed such as oats, wheat, barley, corn and grass and bean was also received and often mixed with supplements. For example, grass enriched with coxford and clover seeds.

Although there was a ready supply locally, some seeds were obtained from further afield. Oat seeds came from Scotland and wheat and barley largely from the Norfolk area.

Animal feed came mainly from Sharpness, Avonmouth and Liverpool Docks. Employee Don Clarke recalls "oats were in bags of half a hundred-weight, barley two, wheat two and a quarter and beans quantities of nineteen stone."

Don Clarke had joined the company at King's Sutton and became one of the first lorry drivers. Others recalled include Alf Tustian, Frank Turvey and Bill Gregory. "We started with two Leyland Cub lorries, each of around 6 or 7 ton capacity. When we moved to Adderbury, we had Leyland Lynx and Vulcan lorries of a similar capacity and by the 1950s fifteen vehicles, largely of Leyland design."

Prior to the transfer to Adderbury, the company had offices in the centre of Banbury and later Bodicote. They also used premises at The Isle of Dogs, East London. "Whilst I am not clear whether the premises were owned by us or not at the time, I do recall driving there during the war and leaving supplies for distribution. It started to get a bit dangerous with the bombing. Some of my trips must have been in about 1944 because the doodlebugs were about."

Whatever the earlier arrangements, by the 1950s the company had taken over the East London premises where it was managed by Tom Roberts who was transferred from Adderbury.

The railway was particularly useful for large consignments, but by the 1950s there was more and more use of lorries, some of which in later years ran up to 200 miles a day.

The manager at King's Sutton was Tom Roberts, who supervised around twelve mill labourers and the lorry driver, but when the company moved to Adderbury, it expanded until there were some 50–60 staff on the payroll.

Potatoes were also distributed from the Adderbury site by a Mr. Barter who apparently leased premises.

Sacks used for the receipt of traffic at Adderbury "were hired through the railway from Hudson, who had depots at Birmingham and Stratford amongst other places, and Gopsill Brown of Gloucester Docks." These sacks were returned to Banbury GWR goods shed for clearance. "Our despatches went in our own sacks – these were hessian whereas the railway ones tended to be heavy duty affairs."

In 1952 a plant breeding department was established in the greenhouses of Adderbury House where grasses, beans and cereals were bred with much success. In 1956 Twyford Vale, an offshoot of Twyford Mill, opened a vegetable processing and packaging plant in the old aluminium factory. The seed breeding operation was moved to King's Sutton in 1966 and was acquired by J. Bibby and Sons Ltd., the well-known animal feed company.

A glimpse of the private siding leading off behind the box to Twyford Seeds' premises.
A. W. DONALDSON

TRAFFIC

COAL MERCHANTS

Charles Wade was the main coal merchant operating from Adderbury station during the 1920s and 1930s. He lived in the village in Back Lane where his premises opened onto the street with a pair of doors. He kept some coal there. He had a driver called Billy West and apparently received about two wagons of coal a week.

He was also a carrier, operating since at least 1911, his Banbury destination being the Leathern Bottle on Mondays, Thursdays and Saturdays.

Charles Wade died in the 1930s, after which the Station wharfage was held by Frosts of Banbury.

Another coal merchant receiving supplies at Adderbury was Ewart Medley of Adderbury West. According to a report of a minor accident, he was using the goods yard in 1943 and owned a motor lorry BKX661.

LIME

Truckloads of lime arrived from Weston-super-Mare for local builder Fred Bray, who picked up supplies from the railway station. On one occasion, the sheet covering the wooden truck had leaked and the lime in the truck caused a fire. It was quenched by throwing water over it.

SAWDUST

Oak sawdust from Wigginton Heath was also supplied to Fred Bray. Oak sawdust was used in the process of steel manufacture.

The back siding was screened from Adderbury House with Arctic Firs planted at the request of the owners. The weighbridge on the left was a 1931 replacement for a smaller cart machine. J. H. RUSSELL

The austere-looking goods shed with its distinctive two-storey office, was another design also repeated at Bloxham and Hook Norton. Again it was built of red brick. The brick parapets of an underline bridge at this point help to give some idea of the embankment at this end of the site, the height of the trackbed above the surrounding fields being far from obvious. P. KARAU

This view, taken c.1947, shows the up and down running lines which extended from the junction with the main line at King's Sutton, the trailing connections to the yard, dock, refuge siding and the private siding which diverged behind the signal box to serve Twyford Seeds. The single-line token set-down post on the left and pick-up post on the right show well here. The boarded crossing over the track was the only means of access to the down platform. J. H. RUSSELL

This timber-built signal cabin at Adderbury was provided in 1905 to replace the original Gloucester Wagon Co. cabin. This structure, classified by the Signalling Record Society as a type 27C, housed a 35-lever stud frame, official dimensions of the locking room being recorded as 25ft x 9ft x 7ft to the operating floor. A. W. DONALDSON

crashed aircraft which arrived by rail. The components were stripped out and separated and the aluminium recovered was melted in a series of furnaces together with virgin aluminium and additional alloys to produce the exacting specification of metal required.

Most of the resulting aluminium billets and ingots were sent to Birmetals Birmingham by road but significant quantities were despatched by rail, signalman Tom Carey recalling the 9.50 p.m. Banbury–Rogerstone train calling at Adderbury for aluminium ingots.

Manned by some 2,300 employees in shifts to cover the 24-hour day, the factory also produced extruded aluminium for the airframes of Lancaster bombers and aluminium powder for flares and incendiaries and was so busy that Bert Lane, who supervised Adderbury, Bloxham and

Without the lavish embellishments of the structure at King's Sutton, the cheaper, more basic execution of the station buildings at Adderbury, Bloxham and Hook Norton gave such a different impression that the common design was far from obvious. Executed in red brick by the impoverished B&C Company, the buildings were very plain and unremarkable, but the curved contour of the canopy valancing did much to enhance their character. Whilst the little waiting rooms were also more plain than King's Sutton, they were at least enclosed. 17th August 1962. C. G. MAGGS

A Kingham to Banbury auto-train alongside the up platform. COLLECTION KIDDERMINSTER RAILWAY MUSEUM

A Kingham-bound auto alongside the down platform in 1951 with just a glimpse of the station master's house on the right. The house was the only one built for a station master on the Banbury to Kingham section. From 1937 it was occupied by Adderbury signalman Tom Carey, who remained there until he retired. W. A. CAMWELL

Collett 2251 class 0–6–0 No. 2259, paired with an ROD tender, approaching Adderbury through Berry Hill cutting with an up goods on 31st December 1955.
COLLECTION A. W. DONALDSON

Hook Norton stations between 1941 and 1949, recalled 100 wagons in the sidings one weekend.

Before the arrival of the factory, 128 tons of general goods were despatched from Adderbury, but the following year this rose to 640 and continued to rise, peaking at 10,545 tons in 1944. Similarly, inward goods tonnage rose from 1,489 in 1941 to a peak of 9,000 tons in 1943. Undoubtedly in connection with the factory, incoming coal rose from 2,691 tons in 1940 to 5,979 in 1941, peaking at 10,024 tons in 1944.

The aluminium factory closed after the war and although it is not clear when the premises were vacated, shortly afterwards they were taken over by Twyford Seeds Ltd whose premises at Twyford Mill, King's Sutton were destroyed by fire. (See panel for details of the company.) It seems that Twyfords' machinery was installed and in operation ready for the autumn trade that year and, whatever the changeover time between the two businesses, the annual figures for general merchandise forwarded and received that year still held at 3,179 and 2,638.

Although the private siding apparently saw limited use for the receipt and despatch of machinery, the station goods yard was used extensively, so much so that the company virtually took it over – "It was easier for us to load and unload with our lorries in the goods yard." When the seed company was established, traffic figures rose again from 5,705 tons of general merchandise forwarded from Adderbury in 1947 to 9,921 tons in 1955 whilst goods received rose from 3,111 in 1947 to 14,476 tons in 1959.

George Turton recalls there was "a hell of a lot of shunting there ... many a time I've come in from Adderbury at teatime, picking up all the box vans loaded with seed for Scotland and elsewhere." With a maximum load of 70 wagons, "we used to run to Banbury Junction and put the train off there so that they could shunt it on to different trains to clear the traffic overnight."

J. H. MOSS

MILTON HALT

85m 42c

A rare view of Milton Halt showing the predictable sleeper-built platform, corrugated-iron pagoda waiting shelter and the less usual provision of a corrugated-iron lamp shed for the storage of paraffin.
COLLECTION ALAN BRAIN

THE opening of a halt at Milton in 1908 was far from unique, but simply part of an extensive programme of providing extra halts all over the GWR system in an attempt to attract passengers from largely rural communities in the face of motor bus competition.

Whether or not those venturing from the little community at Milton provided enough income to yield a profit beyond the establishment, maintenance and running costs of the halt, is difficult to judge because the income from ticket sales was included in the official figures for Banbury station. Furthermore, as with the other stations along this part of the line, local inhabitants recall "there was quite a good bus service through the village".

John Adams, whose family were tenants at Manor Farm from 1940, recalled that his father Bertie put milk on the early train every morning, the milk apparently coming from Tustians farm. As the halt was built on the side of an embankment, close to a bridge spanning a farm track, the only access was by means of a sloping cinder path, which led from a gate adjacent to one of the wing walls of the bridge, up the grass embankment side to the foot of the sleeper-built platform ramp. Manhandling loaded milk churns up the narrow path must have been quite a struggle.

The trimming and refuelling of the lamps at the halt was carried out on Mondays and during his spell at Bloxham in 1937, porter Fred Warren would travel there on his motorbike to trim them. A fuel can was kept in a lock-up store next to the pagoda shelter and Fred recalled that when the supply was running low, he took a four or five gallon can there on the autocar and locked it in the shed. He says that although the Milton lamps were supposed to be emptied out and cleaned every week, the duty was much less frequent in reality.

At such halts it fell to the guards of branch trains to light and extinguish the lamps according to the hours of daylight. Ironically, this means that on miserable days and winter mornings, passengers for the first train had to find their way through the gate, up the cinder path and onto the platform without any illumination. It was not until the train had arrived and they were entering the cosy interior of the autocar, that the guard got off and walked up and down the platform, and perhaps down to the entrance gate, lighting the oil lamps. When extinguishing the lights on the last train at night, the guard would have waited until the passengers were safely off the platform before putting the lights out and departing.

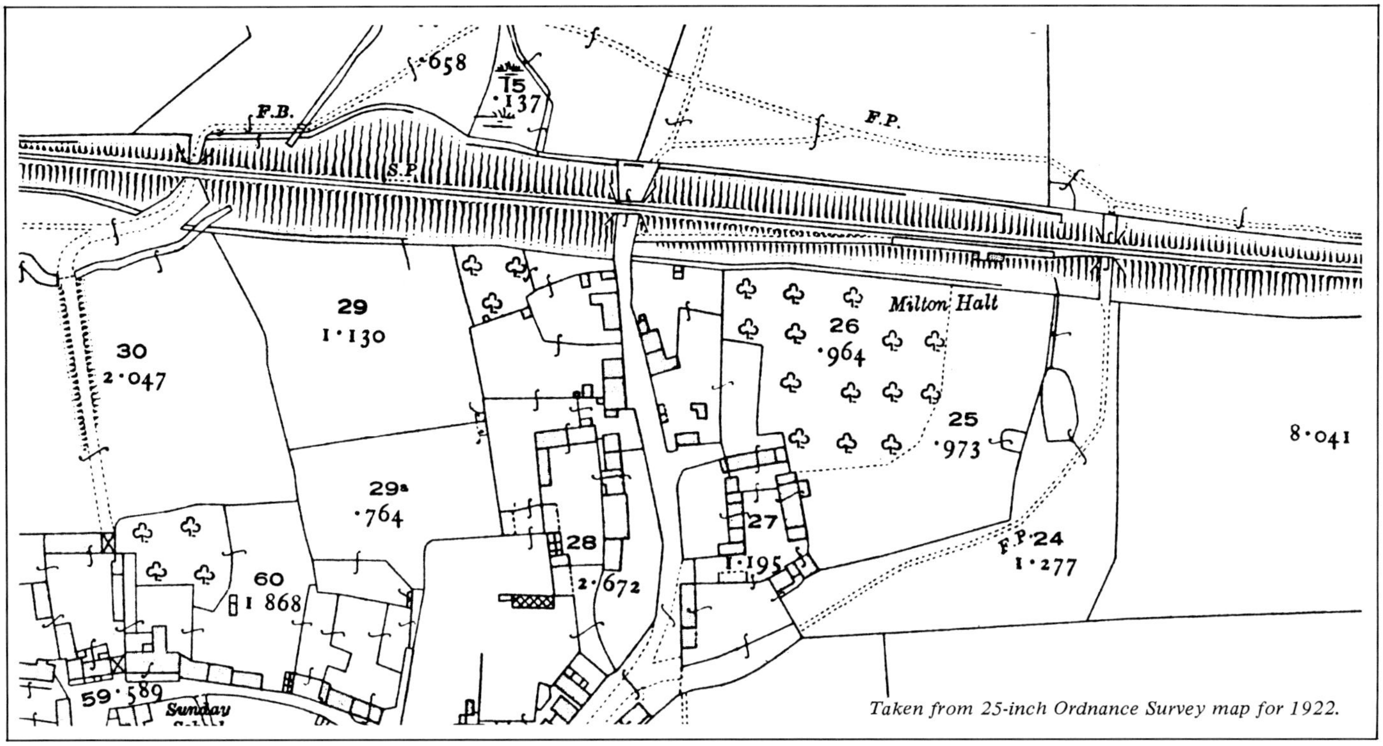

Taken from 25-inch Ordnance Survey map for 1922.

Anothe rare glimpse of the halt with local people Stan Green, Mary Green, Mrs. Chainey, unknown, Bill Bason and Mrs. Bason c.1949.
CTY. N. CHAINEY

The eastern approach to Bloxham station with the brick-arch Barford Road bridge in the background and Dr. Hyde's footbridge c.1952-3. J. H. MOSS

BLOXHAM 87m 14c

Looking west from South Newington road bridge over Bloxham station c.1952-3. The allotment gardens either side of the line are believed to have originated during the war years, but whilst undoubtedly more functional, they could not compare with the 1920s gardens of station master Herbert Lloyd. J. H. MOSS

IN many ways Bloxham station had much in common with Adderbury. It was a quiet wayside station which, from 1918, had a private siding serving local ironstone pits. According to official records for the 1930s, there were only 17–23 tickets sold each week, 12–16 parcels forwarded, 50-60 received, 3–7 tons of general merchandise forwarded, 6–16 tons received and 67–70 tons of coal received. These meagre figures were boosted by the output of the quarry, which probably accounted for approximately 30,000 tons of 'other minerals' forwarded from Bloxham each year.

Unlike Adderbury, however, we are fortunate in having first-hand accounts from four members of staff who worked at Bloxham in the late 1930s and this has enabled us to piece together the routines of a typical day there.

The station staff at this time (1938) were station master William ('Billy') Neale, a Grade 2 porter, a lad porter, a part-time outside porter and two signalmen. William Neale took up the post at Bloxham in 1929, some two years after station master Herbert Lloyd (see Vol. 1 page 176) had moved to Hanborough. Neale lived in 'Clyston', a small detached house in Banbury Road.

During the 1920s, the outside porter was Walter Crook, a self-employed postman who delivered and collected parcels to and from the village and although details are unclear, porter John Hill refers to an outside porter still being there in 1938.

Philip Butt and Harold Hall both became signalmen at Bloxham in 1938, Harold taking the place of Tom White who transferred to Norton Junction, and Philip taking over from Fred Stockford who went to Bewdley. Both Harold and Philip remember when booking on for early turn at 6.0 a.m., the signalman was the only member of staff on duty and dealt with the first train which left Banbury at 6.22 a.m. Philip recalls "there was a locked box near the platform gate and this contained the keys to the station and signal box." In the winter months the first duties were to turn up the oil lights and lay the fires before going to open the signal box. "We issued tickets for the first train, so it was necessary to work between the office and the signal box – they were close so you could hear the bells – there were very few passengers – we might get a few more on Chipping Norton market days."

When the 'Train Entering Section' bell signal for the 6.22 a.m. was received and acknowledged, the electric train staff was released and the signals cleared. The signalman then returned to the booking office and collected the cash bag, which contained the previous day's takings, from the safe. When the train arrived, the train staffs were exchanged and the cash bag placed in the travelling safe which had accompanied the guard from Adderbury en route to the cashier at Worcester. After

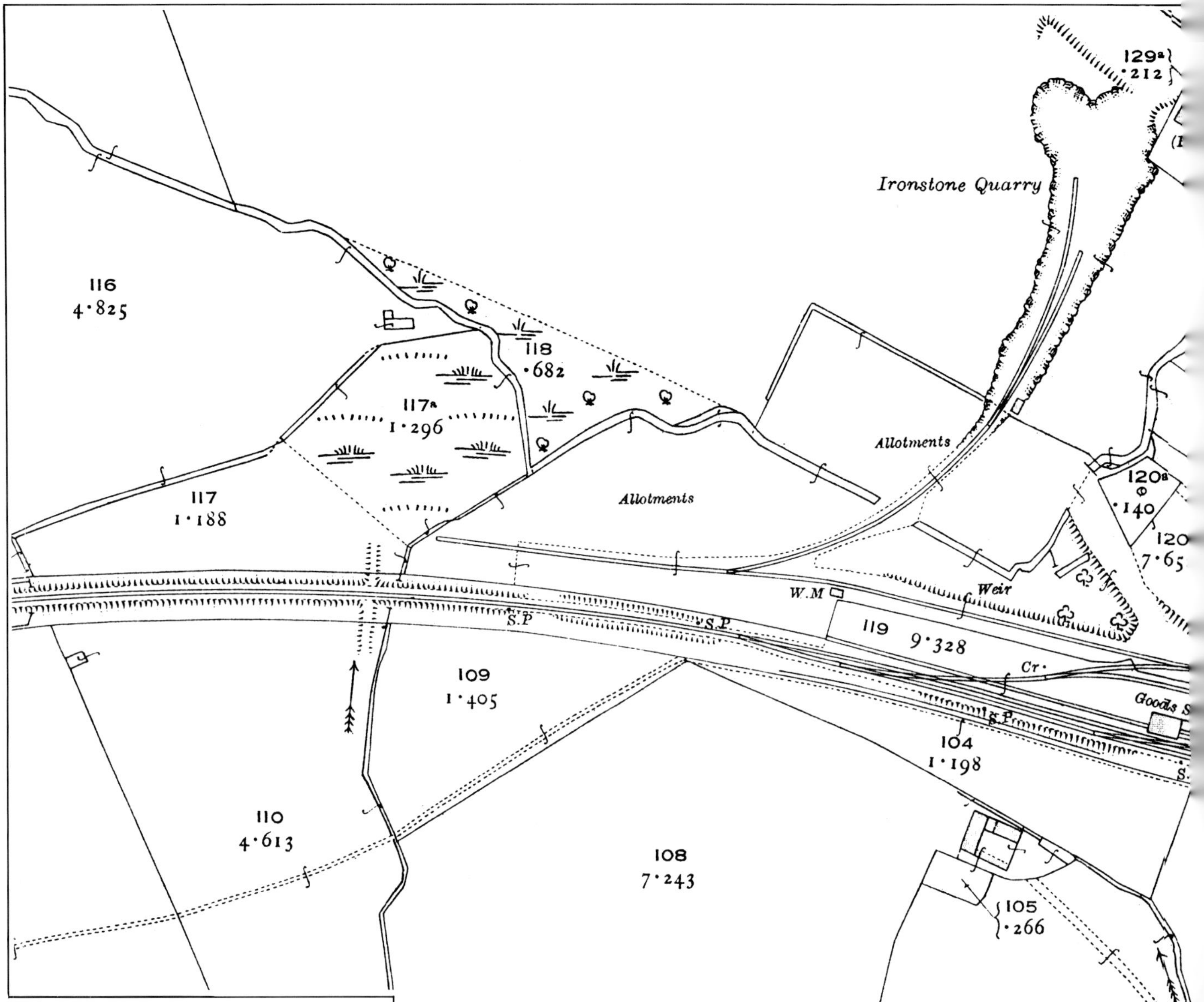

despatching the train at 6.48, the signalman returned to the signal box with the staff to send the 'Train Entering Section' signal to Hook Norton. After this was acknowledged, he replaced the signals and sent 'Train Out of Section' to Adderbury. If necessary, he then returned to the office and later went back to the box to cook breakfast. When the train returned from Kingham at 8.25, Mr. Neale and lad porter Terry Horley had arrived, followed by Grade 2 porter Jack Hill at 9.0.

We haven't tracked down Terry Horley but one of his predecessors, Fred Warren, served at Bloxham for a short period in 1937, travelling from his parents' home at Bledington by motorbike. His hours were 8.0 a.m. to 4.30 p.m. John Hill confirmed signing on duty at 9.0 a.m., the porters' duties beginning with sweeping out and dusting the station buildings. Bloxham is said to have been the only station on the line with lino on the floor. Confined to the booking office, this bounty is believed to have been recovered from Milton Quarries signal box when it closed in 1929. After cleaning the station, the porters went over to the yard to check the wagons for demurrage. Fred said he checked them on the second day and advised the coal merchants to unload their wagons if necessary as the demurrage charges were three shilling per day. He also swept and checked the weighbridge.

The station master covered the office work and booked any passengers. We have already commented on the paucity of tickets sold and in 1938 only 869 tickets were issued, an average of two or three each day, numbers having steadily declined after reaching a peak of some 6,000 in 1913. According to official sources, there was one season ticket holder but the individual is not remembered. As

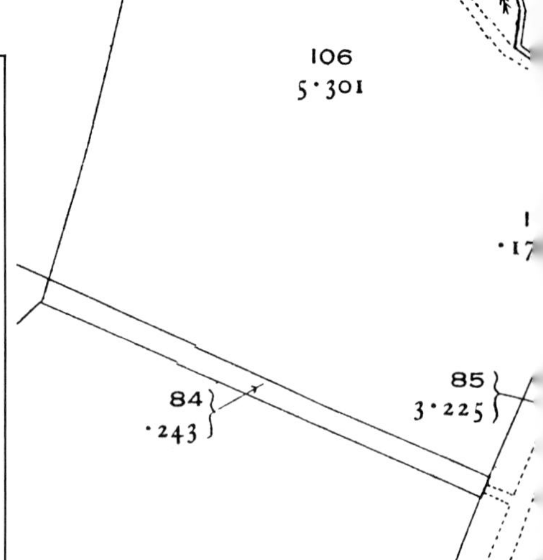

Taken from 25-inch OS map for 1922.

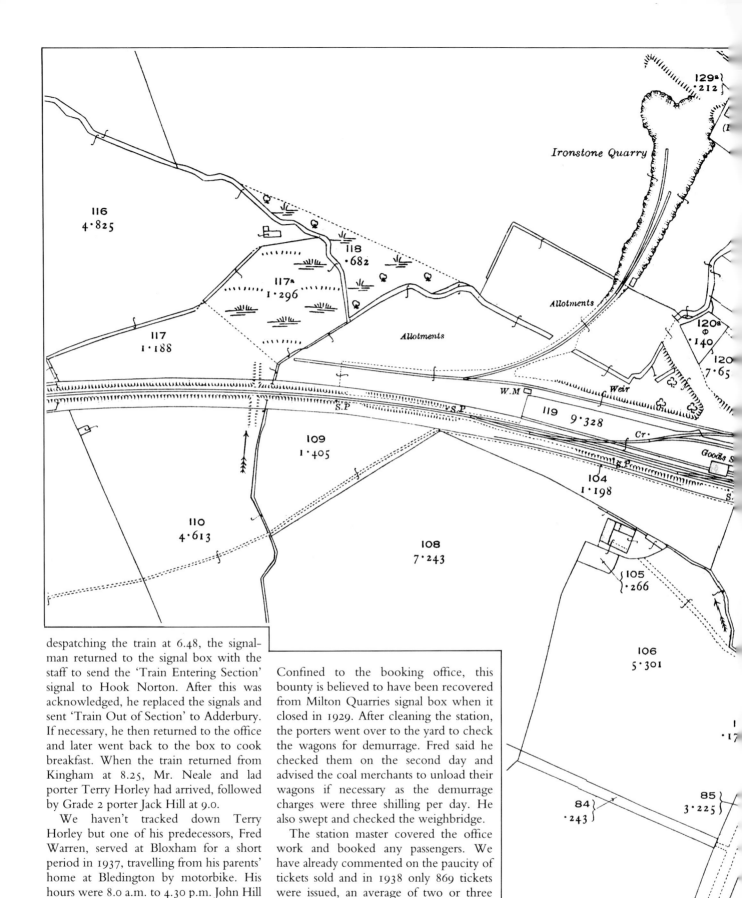

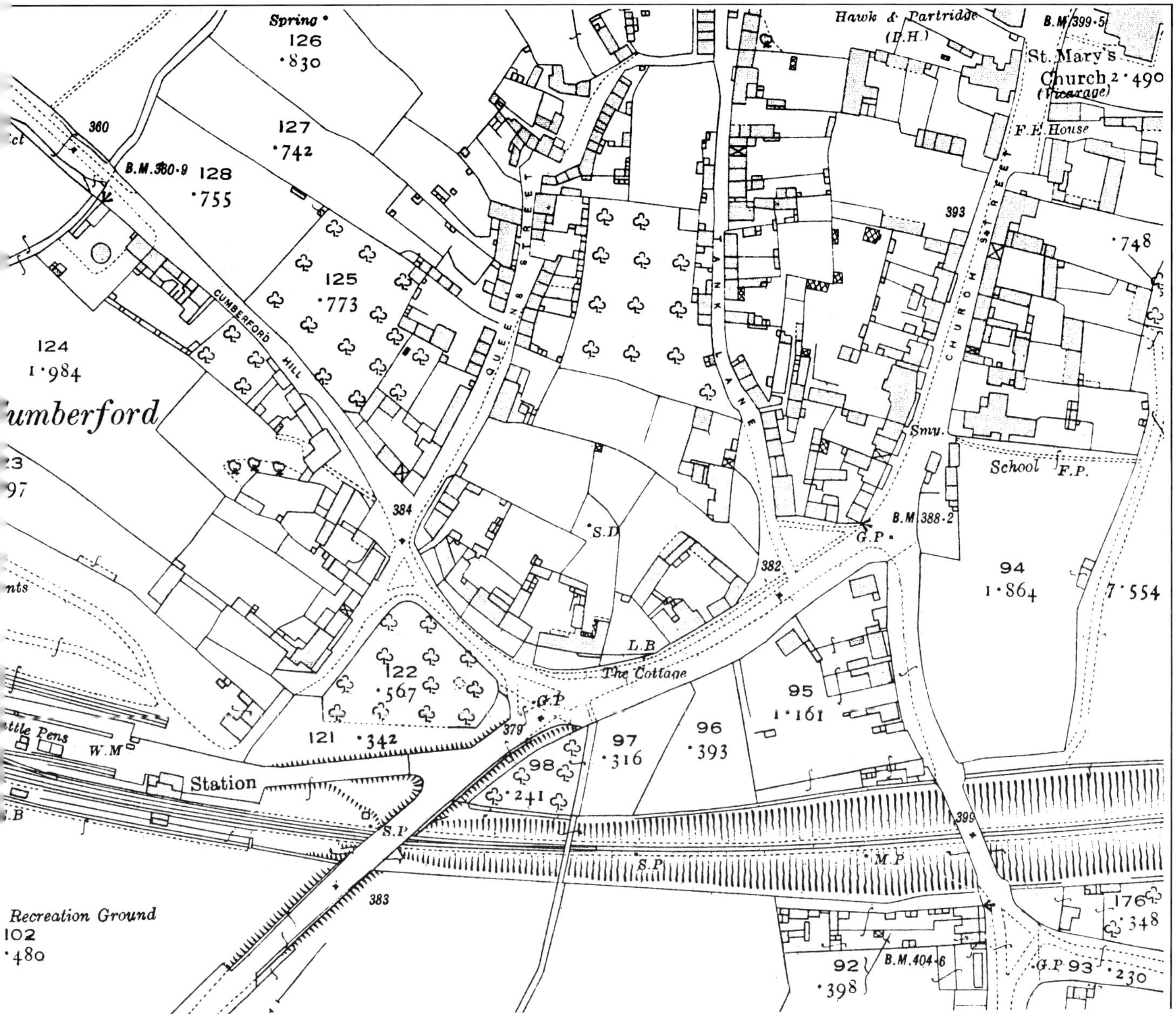

The plate girder bridge carrying the South Newington road, with the up side single-line token pick-up post on the left, one crisp winter's day c.1950. J. H. RUSSELL

Bloxham station in 1951, the cricketers in the background highlighting the close proximity of the adjacent sports field. W. A. CAMWELL

Harold Hall recalled, "It's a wonder we got any passengers at all because the buses were much more convenient – they ran direct to Banbury and were a lot cheaper."

John Hill said the oil lamps at the station were cleaned, trimmed and filled each day, including those at Milton Halt, for which the Bloxham staff were responsible. However, Fred Warren said the lamps were serviced on Mondays.

The porters met each train that arrived and, as there was no footbridge, helped passengers and ferried parcels across the line by means of the boarded crossings at the platform ends. The next Banbury to Kingham auto called at 10.52 a.m.

Parcels were entered into a book where they also were signed for on collection, whilst other parcels were delivered by the outside porter. Archie Warren, who took Jack's place as porter in 1939, recalls delivering small consignments himself, including Lyons cakes to a tuck shop at the other end of the village and "once a week I took supplies to All Saints School". Outside porter Bill Crooks, who worked for two or three days each week, assisted as required, using a flat-bed trolley. "Bill was over age and had been brought back as a supernumary." Reg Manning dealt with any heavy parcels. "I think he had a 30cwt Bedford van."

Incidentally, the signalmen helped out as required with goods and parcels traffic and even did some of the gardening around the station.

When the 10.40 a.m. Banbury to Kingham goods called between 11.30 am. and 12.35 p.m., the porters assisted with shunting.

After arrival in the down platform, the station truck was detached and shunted into the goods shed for unloading – "Sometimes we dealt with it in the down platform – it depended on the nature of the contents. Our traffic was usually immediately behind the station truck." The truck was then returned to the train

Closer views of the up side single-line token set-down post with its leather-clad backboard and the pick-up post.
J. H. RUSSELL

and, with the Bloxham wagons attached, collected outwards wagons and left them on the shed road for the return journey.

Finally, the inwards wagons were positioned in the back road and Ironstone Siding as required. If traffic demanded it, the Clay Cross Ironstone Sidings were served by separate trips from Banbury (which also served Hook Norton). The train continued its journey at 12.35 p.m. after crossing with the 8.15 a.m. Swansea to Newcastle 'Ports to Ports Express', which passed through Bloxham at 12.24 p.m.

The porters were responsible for booking wagons in and out and writing advice notes.

They took it in turn to take an hour for lunch, John Hill recalling that after his lunch he would walk out to the distant signal to check the oil lamp, clean and refill it. During the afternoon, the porters met the Kingham–Banbury autos at 1.6 and 6.5 and the Banbury–Kingham auto at 4.29, booking any parcels into the office and advising addressees where needed. Water for the station lavatories was pumped to fill the reception tank.

"Occasionally, horses and cattle would arrive on the rear of passenger trains, these were disconnected, pushed by hand into sidings and consignees notified by telephone."

The boarded crossing at both ends of the station provided access to the down platform. LENS OF SUTTON

Herbert Lloyd, the station master forever associated with the spectacular station gardens of the 1920s, is seen here c.1924 with the staff of the time. The shorter figure third from left was Walter Crook.
AUTHOR'S COLLECTION

The red-brick station building was entered from the forecourt through a door which opened directly into the general waiting room. The right-hand wall featured only a fireplace which invariably was lit on cold winter days. The left-hand wall had a door leading into the booking office and, to the right of that door, was a ticket window together with the usual wooden rail to guide queuing passengers. The wall facing the main entrance had a padded bench and a single door giving access to the platform. The floor had a lino covering on wooden boards and the walls were decorated with posters advertising excursions and popular holiday destinations in the West Country. When entering the booking office from the waiting room, the facing gable end wall was fitted with a fireplace with a picture over the mantelshelf. To the left was a large duplicating press with a wheeled handle. The left-hand wall had a window overlooking the yard and approach road. The station master's desk was against the opposite wall, in front of the window looking out onto the platform. Here was also the telephone, a bell outside the office under the platform canopy repeating the ring so that station staff could hear it when they weren't in the building. The wall dividing the booking office from the waiting room featured a long counter terminating at the door from the waiting room. Flanking the ticket window were the ticket rack containing pre-printed tickets and the ticket stamping machine. The floor was bare wooden boards. The way out of the general waiting room onto the platform was by a single door whilst another further along on the right gave sole access to the ladies' waiting room, which contained a small table and fireplace and another door leading to the ladies' lavatory. Under the large canopy was the usual bench, a Nestle's chocolate vending machine, and posters on the walls advertising excursions. A clock was fitted beneath the canopy and in the 1920s Herbert Lloyd had hanging baskets of flowers. The wall at the far end had two doors, the one nearest the platform leading into the gents' lavatories with urinals, and pump-operated flushing WC, the second door leading into a store where buckets and cleaning equipment were kept. J. H. RUSSELL

Fred Warren went off duty at 4.30 p.m. and Jack's last job of the day was to collect the empty cash bag off the 5.20 p.m. car from Kingham, which called at Bloxham at 6.5 p.m., and take it to the office ready for the late-turn signalman to fill ready for clearance the next morning.

Mr. Neale was usually there until around 6.0 p.m. and the late-turn signalman who had booked on at 2.0 p.m. dealt with the two evening auto-trains, the Banbury to Kingham, which called at 8.0 p.m., and the return working, which called at 9.35 p.m.

The up goods called between 8.48 and 9.10 p.m. and was scheduled to be overtaken at Adderbury by the 8.55 p.m. autocar from Kingham. As the station staff had gone home, the guard performed the shunting himself. On arrival at Bloxham, the up goods stopped short of the yard where the engine was uncoupled and run forward into the back road to collect any waiting ironstone wagons, which were then attached to the cut of wagons left earlier on the shed road by the down train. The engine then returned to its train and pulled it forward along the up line until alongside the goods shed. Here the engine was uncoupled again and collected the outward wagons through the goods shed via the eastern trailing crossover into the yard.

After the last auto had left at 9.35, the signalman locked up the station and, when the train had gone out of section, he closed the signal box and went home.

Passenger Luggage in Advance was common enough throughout the GWR system, but the beginning and end of terms at All Saints Boys School brought more than enough luggage from its boarding pupils to disturb the quiet daily routine at Bloxham. Fred Warren recalls that at the beginning of term, a lot of the students at Bloxham College never got off at Bloxham but were picked up at Banbury, "yet their luggage always came to Bloxham. We had a van load of luggage arriving on the train and we had a lorry at

Another view of the station on 17th August 1962. C. G. MAGGS

A closer view of the simple brick-built waiting room with its angled canopy/roof. As already mentioned, this was another common design which, besides Adderbury and Hook Norton, could also be found at Chipping Norton. It was much enhanced by the decorative valancing. This view, probably taken on a winter's day c.1950, shows the white-painted corners applied during the Second World War, and what appears to have been a wartime paper label station name used after the removal of main station nameboards. J. H. RUSSELL

54XX 0–6–0PT No. 5404 alongside the down platform with a Banbury to Kingham autocar on 23rd September 1950. F. A. BLENCOWE

Bloxham to deliver it." Conversely, Fred said "The luggage arrived on passenger trains in dribs and drabs – we never had a van back – in fact, most of it was returned by parents when they brought their children back for the start of the next term." At the end of term, certainly in 1938, Fred recalled an empty siphon van came from Banbury and was set back to the shed road by one of the Banbury cars and pinch-barred into the dock. "When the van arrived, we pushed it back so far and allowed it to run into the dock where it was secured." The luggage arrived at the station in a variety of road vehicles, sometimes even farm lorries – "We all mucked in on the loading and usually made some overtime – I recall Farmer Coles of Park Farm gave a hand with his lorry, as did Mr. White, the landlord of the White Lion. When it was ready for despatch, the siphon was barred out to the shed road and collected, usually by the 5.0 p.m. from Kingham, which set back from the platform to fetch it. At Banbury the luggage was transferred to main-line trains.

The outbreak of war brought few changes to the station although, following the retirement of Billy Neale, who had been station master there since 1929, as an economy measure the administration of Hook Norton, Bloxham and Adderbury stations (and Milton Halt) became the responsibility of one station master. The first holder of this post in 1940 was Percy Hiatt, followed three months later by Arthur Kilebie and in 1941 by Bert Lane who remained there until 1949.

When Bert Lane arrived in October 1941 there were only three other staff – signalmen Harold Hall and Fred Warren, and porter Ernie Moulder. Bert recalled that Bloxham wasn't so busy at that period. Nevertheless, the porter's duties increased and new staff were taken on, including a young Bloxham man called Jack Barbour.

Bert's normal routine was to travel from Bloxham to Adderbury in the morning, and return to Bloxham in the early afternoon, probably on the 3.50 Banbury–Kingham train, then visit Hook Norton for the later part of the day, probably travelling up on the 7.50 Banbury–Kingham and finally returning to Bloxham on the 9.20 Kingham–Banbury train. He was also on call on a weekly rotation, from Thursday morning to the following Wednesday night, alternating with William Williams, the Chipping Norton station master.

Since the outbreak of war, the signalling duties had changed from the usual eight-hour shifts of 6.0 a.m.–2.0 p.m. and 2.0 p.m.–10.0 p.m. and became a more tiring twelve-hour 6.0 a.m.–6.0 p.m. and 6.0 p.m.–6.0 a.m.

This arrangement enabled the signal boxes to maintain twenty-four hour cover to allow the branch to remain open to the possibility of troop train manoeuvres and as an alternative route in the event of another line being obstructed.

Troop trains, incidentally, were uncommon visitors to the line. Fred recalled only one stopping at Bloxham during a night shift in the three years he was there.

To help ease the burden of the 12-hour shifts, relief signalman Gordon Keeling transferred from Torquay. He worked a one week in three duty of an eight-hour shift with the other two weeks being twelve-hour shifts on the Banbury–Kingham line, day turns only, initially at Bloxham and Adderbury, but later on, Hook Norton was also included.

For Harold and Fred, the night shift must have been a lonely and tedious duty in wartime, with the signal boxes blacked out to avoid recognition by the pilots of enemy aircraft. On the Banbury–Kingham line this usually took the form of simply dimming the signal box lights. At Bloxham, Harold went one better by making a set of blinds from stiff paper to conceal the signal box windows. As Fred recalled, "We just pulled the blinds down and you wouldn't know that a signal box was there."

The two signalmen worked opposite turns. Harold worked the early shift, which was convenient because he and his wife Ellen lived close by, renting Frank Coppage's cottage in Queen Street, a short distance from the station. Fred usually took the afternoon shift, driving to the station from Banbury in his Austin Seven.

One afternoon, at around 6.0 p.m., Fred Warren had a surprise when he entered the station approach road in his car, ready to relieve Harold for the night turn. During the afternoon and without

Looking east through the station during the final years. L&GRP

any forewarning, the Durham Light Infantry had entered the station with a field artillery gun and taken command of the goods shed, holing up in the loft above the goods office, 'up the wooden ladder', the plan being to commandeer the improvised base for the next 21 days.

Fred explained: "I came belting down the road in my Austin Seven, the gate was always left open. When I got there, half a dozen soldiers were round there." One approached Fred suspiciously, saying, "Didn't you see the bloke at the gate?" "No, I did not", replied Fred. The soldier said, "You could have got shot."

Fred saw that Harold was coming off duty and the soldiers were continuing to bar his way. He admitted he was starting to feel annoyed at their intrusion and told them, "If you don't let me through there, you won't get any trains tonight", whereupon they did!

In 1942 Bert Lane's wife Beatrice joined the staff at Bloxham station as a booking clerk. As Bert recalled: "Going out to work was a bit strenuous". Beatrice had been concerned about the health of her ageing mother. An agreement was made that she could leave the railway at the earliest convenient opportunity. As it was, she enjoyed the varied nature of her work, recalling that "railway clerks did all sorts of things then"; she remained at Bloxham until the war was over.

Bert and Beatrice travelled to Bloxham on the 7.50 Kingham–Banbury train, and now that he had his wife's assistance, instead of travelling home from Hook Norton on the last train, they both travelled home to Chipping Norton on the 3.50 Banbury–Kingham.

A closer view of the station building, showing the recessed centre section of the platform elevation and also showing the two doorways in the western end gable wall. COLLECTION S. BOLAN

With Beatrice to assist, the supervision arrangements for Adderbury, Bloxham and Hook Norton altered somewhat, with Bert spending two days a week at each station, beginning at Hook Norton, and visiting all three on the last day of the month to pay the wages to his salaried staff.

In the middle war years, more staff arrived, Bert taking on Mrs. Dorothy Gibberd to carry out porter's duties with Terry Horley. Ernie Moulder was transferred to Adderbury.

As described previously, one of the essential porters' duties was to refuel the signal lamps, taking them to the signalman to trim them first. However, for some reason Mrs. Gibberd was excused this particular duty. It says something about the easygoing way in which the stations were run that the duty often fell to Bert Lane to replace the signal lamps, with Mrs.

The signal box was a standard GWR design built in 1907 to replace the original timber-built Gloucester Wagon Co. cabin just apparent in the photos on page 105 of Volume 1. According to official records, this box was re-assembled from Bays Hill, Cheltenham, where redevelopment had made it redundant. The recorded dimensions of the locking room are 23ft 10in x 12ft x 8ft and the frame was a 29-lever stud frame with 5¼in spacing. The small corrugated-iron building on the left was used as a lamp shed whilst the sleeper-built hut beyond was a platelayers' hut.
J. H. MOSS

The front elevation of the signal box viewed from the goods yard.
COLLECTION S. BOLAN

A closer view of the single-line token catcher with its padded leather backboard, seen here c.1950. J. H. RUSSELL

Gibberd standing at the bottom, looking up and anxiously calling, "Are you alright, are you alright?" Women had begun to be employed in the signal boxes on the line around 1944. Both Adderbury and Hook Norton were covered in this way, to release men to be employed in the war effort. Winnie Marshall, daughter of Banbury engineman Wally Marshall, was at Adderbury. Madge West, the daughter of a Banbury signalman, was trained for signal box duties and, after passing her rules examinations in Worcester, she began at Bloxham on the opposite shift to Harold Hall on an eight-hour 6.0 a.m.–2.0 p.m. and 2.0 p.m.–10.0 p.m. rotation. Madge viewed her Bloxham appointment and those of the other women with practicality: "We felt we were doing our part for the war effort."

Madge West remained at Bloxham until 1945. Travelling by bicycle to and from work at night was not always pleasant, as she explained, "Sometimes in the bad weather I was there until 11 o'clock waiting for the last train to come back from Kingham. I then had to cycle back to Banbury, often getting checked for identification by the American army who were stationed at Wykham Park during the war."

Twenty years had passed since Herbert Lloyd lovingly created and tended the

The red-brick goods shed was similar to the one at Adderbury and was equipped with a 1½ ton fixed hand crane FM840, the goods office was approached down a flight of steps from the loading platform. Cattle were often handled at Bloxham, cattle vans being brought in as tail loads on the rear of the Banbury to Kingham autocar. Tail loads on down trains were set back over the trailing crossover from the down loop, then positioned by hand whilst traffic on up trains were set back onto the shed road via the crossover in the foreground, then pinch-barred to the dock behind the platform. J. H. MOSS

Another view of the platelayers hut, the token pick-up post and the shed used to store the gangers trolley, the boarded crossing enabling the trolley to be man-handled onto either up or down tracks. COLLECTION S. BOLAN

beautiful station gardens, and Bert Lane admitted when he was interviewed many years later that in his time "they weren't so good". During the austere times of the Second World War the Bloxham gardens were transformed into a series of allotments. Harold Hall planted rows of tomatoes between the booking office and the signal box. As Fred Warren recalled, "They were beautiful. We used to have a few cattle that came in, and the manure from the pens used to go on the tomatoes." In a two-yard piece near the signal box, between the railway and the boundary fence, Fred planted brussells sprouts which the stopping goods driver Tommy Thornton used to buy, and in the Hook Norton direction, Fred grew potatoes. Bert also took a piece of land between the station building and the road bridge. The permanent way men were equally resourceful, keeping the staff regularly supplied with rabbits. Once a week Harold bought a crate of fish, which he had ordered from Grimsby and sold on to the station staff as they required it.

If more local people used the railway during the war years, then it is not recalled by the Bloxham staff. The fact that Colonel Woods and Mrs. Hawtin were remembered as occasional travellers points to the rarity of locals, so it is not difficult to imagine the sharp contrast when hordes of RAF personnel based at Barford St. John descended on the station to buy tickets for the 6.5 p.m. train to Banbury. As the last train from Banbury arrived back at 8.0 p.m., they bought 8d singles and found alternative transport to get them back later. On Thursdays and Saturdays, they made almost exclusive use of the late Banbury to Bloxham train which was an extension of the Banbury–Kingham roster introduced in 1939. This train arrived in Bloxham at 10.45 p.m. The return fare was 1 shilling and fourpence, although the armed services travelled half price. The RAF evidently made a dramatic effect on the number of tickets issued and in 1944 this peaked at 5,904.

As the war drew to an end, various staff changes occurred: Madge West left the signal box. Ernie Moulder, who had been posted to Adderbury as a porter, served part-time at Bloxham and Adderbury, travelling in to Bloxham by bus from Hook Norton and taking the first train to Adderbury at 8.30 a.m., returning on the 4.10 p.m. from Banbury between

The 20-ton weighbridge No. 7298 with its timber office seen here in the final years. According to a 1938 listing, the plate measured 18ft x 8ft. Hay merchant Roland Newton from Barford had loads weighed here and P. G. Hirons timber merchants, founded in 1948, paid 2s 3d each time they had their lorry loads weighed there. All their timber was delivered by road.
COLLECTION S. BOLAN

GOODS TRAFFIC

OUTWARDS

Hay – In common with other local stations, hay was dealt with by agent Roland Newton of Hook Norton, who organised delivery to the station by Reg Manning, a Bloxham carrier, using a blue 30cwt lorry. He lived in the High Street. Sheeting and roping were the responsibility of railway staff – "We usually used the yard or shed road – incidentally, Newton was very fussy – we had to use three sheets, one in the middle with two outer ones."

Wheat – Quantities of wheat were sent out by local farmers in the season. Packed in 2¼cwt sacks and dealt with by Silcock and Hudson, it was sent to Avonmouth Docks in box vans. "If these were not available, we used sheeted opens – we used to get about a week's notice of the traffic."

Timber – Fred Warren remembers Claridges of Heythrop sending out the occasional load – this was one of the few times we used the yard crane."

INWARDS

Coal

Welford – supplies for this Oxford-based firm were dealt with by Bert Heath, who had an office near the cattle pens. "Coal was bagged direct in the back road but Bert also had a dump at the other end of the yard alongside the spur, and wagons were pinch-barred in and out of here from the back road." Coal supplies were delivered by Albert Springhall who is remembered as "a polite old gent". Bert Johnson also covered some deliveries.

Palmer – This was a Banbury company who had a local agent, Walter Crook, later Walter Cannings, with an office near the weighbridge. Bert Hawtin handled their deliveries using a horse and cart.

Johnson – Bert Johnson initially acted as agent for Palmer and apparently later took over when he retired.

Tar

Sheeted open wagons of tar are remembered arriving at Bloxham for the construction of Barford Aerodrome, which appears to have started in 1939. This was collected by contractors' staff who unloaded it in the yard road. At the airfield the tar is said to have been deposited directly on top of grass to form the runways.

Wagons of livestock

"Cattle arrived regularly from Gloucester Market for farmer Colgrave on the back of the last car from Kingham. They were backed into the yard and detached in the same way as the school luggage van. We also had a cattle wagon from Stow Market pretty regularly and this was left beside the pens in the same way. It came in on the last car from Kingham on Saturday, so the cattle stayed in the wagon overnight – one of the porters came on Sunday morning to supervise the unloading. I believe they were collected by a trader from the Milcombe area." Eighty-five wagons of livestock were handled in 1938 – around one or two each week.

Adderbury and Bloxham before going home to Bloxham on the 6.0 p.m. bus

At the unashamed risk of a little duplication, Harold Hall's recollections of Bloxham station in 1946 provide an insight to the immediate postwar years. Harold had seen many signalling staff work his opposite turns since he was transferred there from Adlestrop in 1938. Initially, Harold had lodged in Hook Norton, cycling the six miles to Bloxham and soon after, in 1939, he and his wife Ellen leased retired Hook Norton station master Frank Coppage's cottage on Queen Street, where they remained during the nine years Harold was at the station.

Harold was the first to arrive at the station at 6.20 a.m. The walk to the station was quick, because he took a short cut through the lane past the cottages where 'Durg' Hawtin and Sybil Tyrrell lived, climbed over a stile at the end and entered the railway yard near the weighbridge. Harold unlocked the signal box with the key which he kept, switched in, tested the instruments and checked that the tokens were free and in place.

The forecourt elevation of the station building, seen from the weighbridge. COLLECTION S. BOLAN

The first train to arrive was the 6.20 a.m. from Banbury. Harold took the token from the machine and handed it to the fireman, together with the cash bag, which he'd taken from the office safe, and placed it safely within the cash box in the vestibule of the autocoach. This had come up from Worcester on the 5.20 p.m. Kingham train of the previous day, arriving at 6.0 p.m. The porter had taken the cash box out and put it on a barrow in the waiting room.

Once the train had been given the 'all clear' to proceed to Hook Norton, Harold pulled off the signals and crossed the boarded crossing to the booking office. He unlocked the door to the office and the safe, removed the cash bag and placed it in the cash box, which he then wheeled over to the train. The guard, regularly Mrs. Beer from Banbury on the early turn, then took responsibility for it en route to Kingham, where the cash box was transferred to the Worcester train. (Originally, the cash box was taken to Adderbury, being the furthest station on the route in the Worcester division, but the procedure was altered around 1937.)

The Bloxham permanent way gang arrived at around 7.30 a.m., having booked on duty at Hook Norton where the trolley was stowed. The journey down took half

The end loading dock behind the up platform. COLLECTION S. BOLAN

Looking east through the station from the goods yard with the dock siding on the left.
C. F. D. WHETMATH

Left: *The corrugated-iron roofed hut behind the sleeper-built coal pen was Welford's coal office. Inside was a desk and a coal-burning stove together with a sleeper-built platform which the agent Bert Heath had made up to rest on when there was a lull in business. As a boy in the mid-1920s, Arthur Hosband, Bert's nephew, helped out with coal wharf duties. In winter months, he recalled, Bert would "get a fire on the stove and it used to roast you to death". Outside the office was a lean-to coal bunker which had a chute by which coal was fed into his stove. They bagged, weighed and loaded up together. Bert usually shovelled and Albert held the bags and weighed them on the cart weighing machine. The coal merchants were charged a levy by the Great Western Railway for use of the weighbridge. Loading the horse-drawn dray took 45 minutes and once it was ready, the delivery man, Albert Springall, drove off down the village while Bert went back to the office and would record the quantity of coal which had been taken. He was also on hand to sell coal direct to villagers who would arrive with a two-handled truck or barrow. Delivery of the coal took half a day and if Albert returned before 4.0 p.m., he would load up for the following day's work. Otherwise he would finish his duties by stabling the dray by the side of the wall at the top of Tank Lane and taking 'Duke', the 18-hand shire horse, for a well-earned exercise session in one of farmer Mark Mawl's fields on Tadmarton Road. The horse was kept in the fields throughout summer weekends and stabled during the week, whereas in winter months it was stabled all the time it wasn't required.* Right: *The cattle pen, situated on the loading dock. Certainly in the 1930s, coal merchant Palmer had an office behind the pens. This is said to have been yellow in colour and constructed of asphalt sheeting.*
COLLECTION S. BOLAN

an hour. All the gang were made up of Hook Norton men. Incidentally, during extremely icy weather, one of the platelayers, Freddie Rolfe, from Milcombe, was allocated the task of applying salt to keep the points free, often attending from morning until night.

Harold took breakfast around this time and in between trains he studied a correspondence course in passenger and parcels traffic, the theoretical questions being set from the Divisional Office in Worcester. As it was quiet, there would be the opportunity to just walk around.

The early-turn porter arrived at 8.0 a.m. In 1946 this duty was carried out by Gerald Johnson, who had been taken on by Bert Lane in January of that year. His duties finished at 5.0 p.m. The first job was to light the fire in the hearth of the ticket office. (No other fire was lit.) Afterwards Gerald sorted parcels for distribution round the village. Some had arrived on the passenger and others came via the van on the previous day's pick-up goods. The parcels were delivered by lad porter Terry Horley by bicycle, or on a sack truck. The college regularly ordered a large box of ice cream, which Terry took up to Mrs. Little's shop.

Monday was the day that the traditional lamping duty was carried out. According to Gerald, it took nearly all day to trim them, fill them and take them back out. The paraffin and spare lamps were kept under the signal box. Two lamps were provided for every signal to ensure that one was ready filled. The spare lamps were filled as a separate duty. The platform lamps were also included in Monday's duty, but for some reason those at Milton Halt were omitted.

Livestock was occasionally transported from Bloxham; Colonel Woods of Bloxham was a frequent user, transporting horses by rail from the station. Captain Carter from Barford also transported horses from the station. He was a breeder and sent his mares during season. Horseboxes were ordered two days in advance, a duty which Bert Lane administered. Gerald recalled that Captain Carter led them in to the station on the hoof, and Gerald would lead the horse in to the box loose, supplied with plenty of bedding. There was always a tip at the end of it and the manure was welcome – Gerald spread it over his allotment.

Working with livestock was not always straightforward. Bert Lane's wife Beatrice remembered that during her time helping in the booking office, a dealer from Milcombe brought two horses into the

BLOXHAM IRONSTONE TRAFFIC

Ironstone workings are detailed in Volume Three but this brief summary is intended to support the operational details of the private siding.

Ironstone pits off the Tadmarton Road were started by the Northampton Ironstone Co. in 1918, a 270 yard standard gauge tramway connecting the workings to a private siding on the northern edge of the goods yard at Bloxham station. In 1925 the company went into liquidation, but two years later the Clay Cross Co. took over the workings, employing some 12–20 men and a small steam engine to ferry wagons between the pits and the GWR station.

The Ironstone Company's own engine collected empties from the back siding of the goods yard and delivered the loaded ones so that the Great Western engine did not have to enter the private siding from which it was prohibited. Small numbers of wagons were conveyed in the regular goods trains but larger quantities were handled by dedicated ironstone trains run if traffic demanded them. The summer 1939 service timetable shows a 2.5 p.m. Banbury to Hook Norton returning at 4.40 p.m., calling at Bloxham in both directions. The timetable also shows a 2.30 p.m. Banbury Ironstone sidings to Margam which called at Bloxham from 3.16 to 3.31 pm., but signalman Archie Warren remembers a train from Banbury only serving Bloxham in the morning – "This train arrived in the up loop and left the brake van to place the empties. When the loco came out, it ran via the down loop to the other end of the brake and returned to Banbury. When working back, it came out in the afternoon as engine and brake and left the brake in the same way while collecting the loaded wagons, which were left on the down loop. The brake van was then attached to the rear and the loco ran round for the return." Signalman Philip Butt remembers "the outward train arrived about 12.40 p.m. and a return ran at around 5.40 or 6.40 p.m." but doubtless these were adjusted to suit local requirements.

Archie Warren recalls that in the late 1930s as many as 18 wagons were dealt with each day.

The pit was closed in 1942, but after the war it was re-opened on a smaller scale with just three men but modern equipment in 1947. This yielded approximately 18,000 to 26,000 tons a year before the pit was finally wound up in 1954.

Looking towards the station c.1950 with the goods yard on the left. The spur in the left-hand corner of the photograph served Welford's coal yard and storage area. The Clay Cross Works were on the far left. J. H. RUSSELL

Churchward Mogul No. 5391 shunting a down freight at Bloxham during the early 1950s.
F. A. BLENCOWE

station to be taken by rail to Banbury. The team at Bloxham loaded the horses, 'barred' the wagons, to the goods shed, including the horse-box, ready to drop onto the train when it arrived. Mrs. Beer, the ever-efficient guard, checked the destination on the wagon label and got inside, calling out, 'One horse, Mr. Lane'. Bert knew they had loaded two, and said, "If there's only one, the other one's got out." He climbed in and checked the van Sure enough, the horse was there, upside-down in the hay with its legs in the air, struggling to get up With great urgency, the van was shunted back to the dock and the other horse removed. Bert clambered in to release the rope tying the horse back to the head-stall and the animal got up, after which Beatrice led it round the yard. Bert was sure the horse would have been dead by the time the train had reached Banbury.

Cattle were less frequent. Stroud's sent some by rail occasionally, as did Colegrave's of Wyckham Lane. Usually two cattle vehicles were ordered, which arrived from Worcester. Up to six head of cattle could be accommodated in each. Gerald recalled that on occasions when the cattle were stopped overnight in the pens, the porters would go down and give them water. The porters also cleaned the vehicles before they were returned.

The daily pick-up goods arrived at 11.0 am. Often the parcels van would be detached and left in the goods shed overnight. The principal traffic received, of course, was coal. Welford's coal merchants still retained wharfage at Bloxham station, but Bert Heath had left around the time that war broke out. The station agent was Charlie Faulkner. In 1948 the duty was taken by Fred Timms whose career had begun at Bloxham station as a porter in 1947. He worked as Welford's agent for eight years. A private coal merchant was operating in place of Palmers which by that time was run by Bert Johnson.

Clay Cross were operating from Bloxham, the last of the Banbury and Cheltenham linked companies to remain in operation. During the war, between six and eight trucks a day were dispatched from there. Later, production eased off (see separate panel).

Gerald Johnson's position as a porter did not last long, and soon a vacancy arose in the signal box, which suited him. Promotion occurred more rapidly during that period than for many years. He applied himself to learning all the rules by heart.

Harold and Gerald worked opposite turns. Between them they set to work cleaning the signal box, restoring its former appearance after the wartime years of neglect. As Gerald described it: "We burnished the levers, polished the floor and black-leaded the fire grate of the stove. We tidied up the flower beds, which hadn't been touched during the war. It took the best part of a year to get it back to how it looked before. We scrubbed the waiting rooms up and polished the thick brown lino."

One year later, Harold Hall left, after nine years at Bloxham. In 1947 he was promoted to Grade 2 Relief 2nd Class signalman covering up to four signal boxes in the Worcester Division, based at Kingham.

A final view of Bloxham from the Kingham end. COLLECTION S. BOLAN

COUNCIL HILL SIDINGS 90m 59c

COUNCIL Hill Sidings, which served the Brymbo Ironstone Works, trailed from the up direction, therefore empties from Banbury had to be taken past to Hook Norton station where the engine could run round and take them back. The various ironstone workings along the line are detailed in Volume Three, but as the Brymbo Works survived until 1945 and were integral with the operation of Hook Norton station, we have featured the sidings here. Former porter Harold Hall recalled that in his time, 1927–29, no ironstone traffic went from here via Kingham.

The entrance to the private sidings was marked by a large gate which it was the porter's duty to open and close later after the train had gone. As mentioned in the station account, the porter rode out from Hook Norton in the brake van.

On arrival at the sidings, the brake van was detached and, after the porter had collected the single-line train staff from the driver, the empty wagons were drawn forward clear of the points. Using the key on the end of the staff to unlock the lever frame, the porter operated the points and signalled the train back into one of the three loop sidings where the guard and the porter secured the wagons which were then left for the ironstone staff to gravitate down into the works for loading as required.

The engine then ran over to the loading siding to collect the loaded wagons which had been checked over by a GWR wagon examiner called 'Tapper' who, stationed at Bloxham, was responsible for inspecting the ironstone wagons at both the Bloxham and Hook Norton workings. The loaded wagons were hauled out of the sidings and after the porter had closed the gates and restored the points, they were propelled back along the running line and coupled onto the waiting brake van.

The porter handed the single-line staff back to the driver, then telephoned the signalman at Hook Norton for instructions. If there was time for the train to reach Bloxham, it was given permission to proceed and the porter would walk back to the station. However, if there was no time to clear the section before the next train was due, the Hook Norton signalman would put out a special 2–5 signal and the train was propelled back to the station where it was put into the ironstone sidings behind the down platform. The single-line staff was returned to the signalman who cancelled the 2–5 signal and the ironstone train remained there until there was a clear passage towards Banbury.

Finally, an official report of a derailment at 5.35 p.m. on Boxing Day 1941 provides a snapshot of one of the ironstone trains at the sidings:

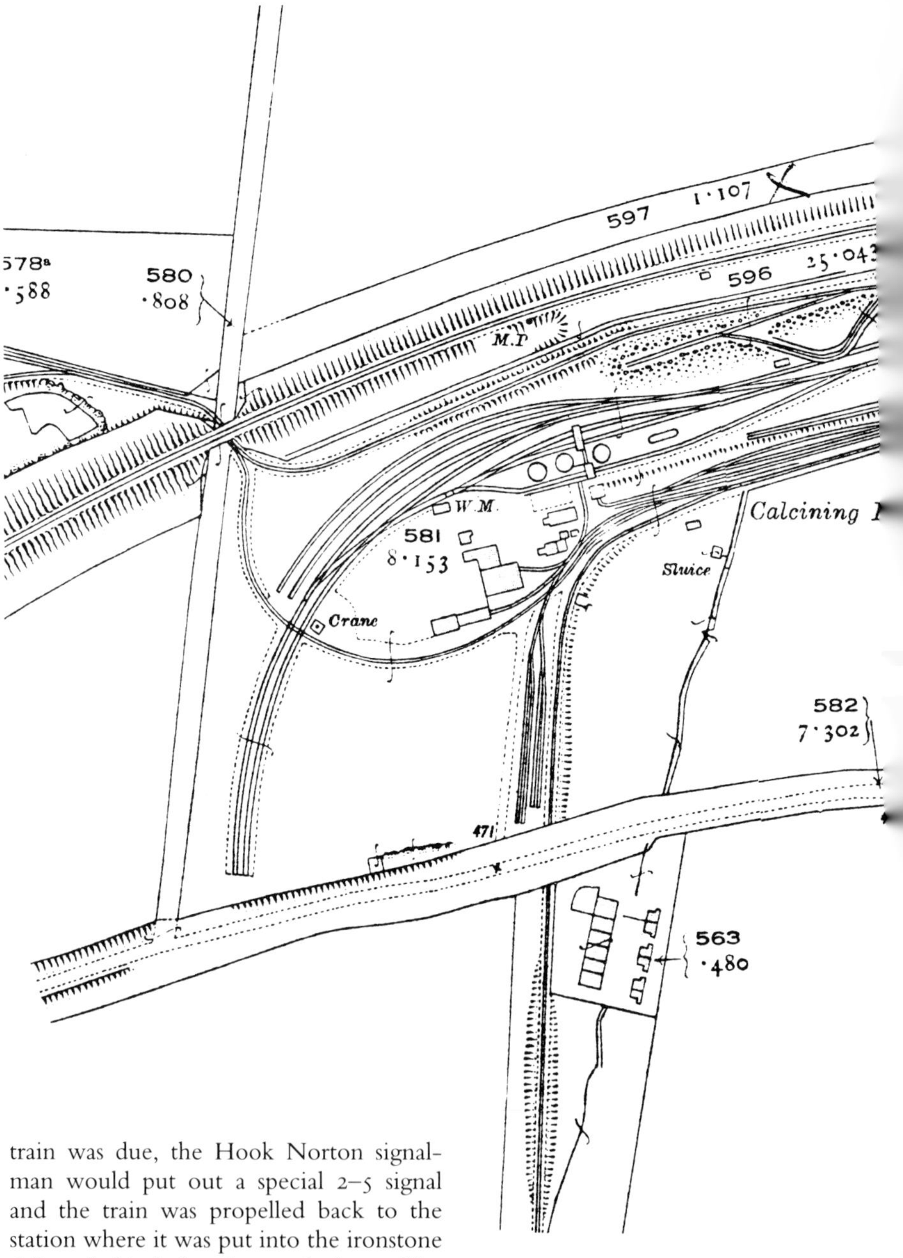

'As Engine 2378 (4.40 p.m. Hook Norton to Banbury) was drawing fifteen wagons of iron ore from the Council Hill Sidings towards the running line, the engine struck the toe of a pair of hand points and became derailed one pair of wheels.

'The Banbury breakdown vans were requisitioned 5.48 p.m., arrived 8.45 p.m. and the engine was rerailed at 9.50 p.m.

'The derailment did not foul the running line but the brake van had been left thereon and the 5.10 p.m. Auto Car ex Kingham was utilised to remove it from the section under the provisions of Regulation 14.'

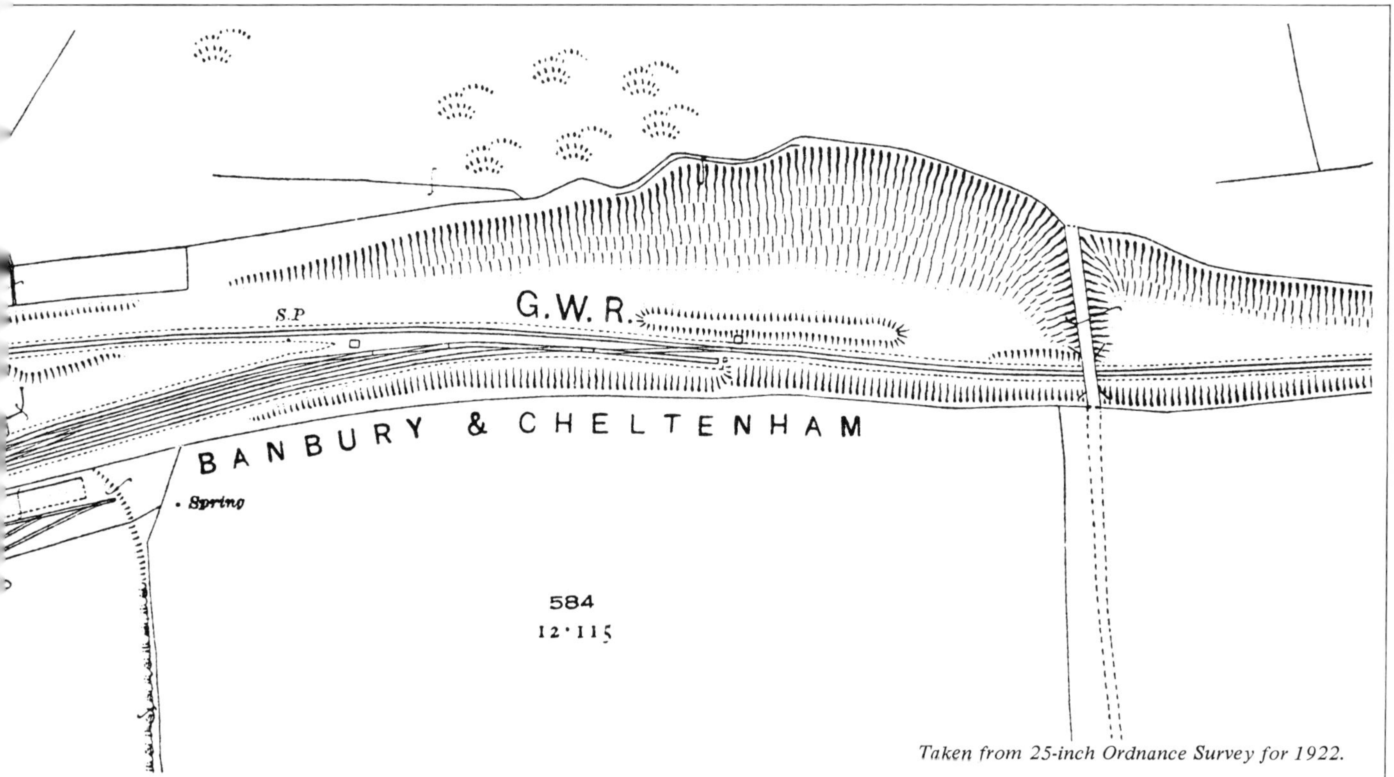

Taken from 25-inch Ordnance Survey for 1922.

The ironstone works at Council Hill. Further details of this and other ironstone workings will appear in Volume 3.

F. R. PACKER, CTY. ALAN BRAIN

HOOK NORTON

91m 37c

64

This picture, looking in the up direction towards Banbury with the lengthening shadows of a spring evening in 1947, was probably taken from the post of the lamp illuminating the single-line token catcher. It almost represents the signalman's view and shows the trailing connection to the ironstone sidings behind the down platform, the deck of the skewed plate girder span over the Banbury road, the up starting signal, up advanced starting signal and the down home. In the right distance we can see the calcining kilns of Brymbo Ironworks at Council Hill which was served by a private siding trailing from the up direction.

J. H. RUSSELL

The flower beds, traditionally edged with whitewashed stones, and recently whitewashed platform edge are evidence of the pride in the station's appearance at that time. This picture is said to have been taken in the 1920s. F. R. PACKER

Of the places served by the Banbury & Cheltenham Railway, perhaps Hook Norton, more than any other, encapsulated the spirit of the enterprise, for here in this corner of north-west Oxfordshire the two characteristics which most clearly defined the railway were evident. Here were the largest concentrations of ironstone deposits, the very reason for the railway, and here, too, were the major engineering features which were instrumental in bringing the railway to the heart of the ironstone fields. Both elements completely transformed the environment – the industrial engineering encompassed in the massive kilns and equipment which accompanied the ironstone production, and the civil engineering involved in the construction of the two massive viaducts, embankments and tunnel.

Apart from the direct loops built at Hatherley and Chipping Norton Junction in 1905, the building of the viaducts represented the last important elements in the sequence of events to construct the railway. In viewing these grand structures, one can appreciate the tremendous effort which was expended on their construction and recognise a sense of the pioneering spirit which the promoters of the railway carried with such single-minded determination.

The ironstone workings are detailed in Volume Three but for the purpose of these notes are summarised as follows. During the 1930s the ironstone workings at Hook Norton were confined to the pits of the Brymbo Ironstone Co. at Council Hill, just east of the station. The output between 1935 and 1939 varied between 23,916 tons (478 tons per week) in 1938 and 83,441 (1,668 tons per week) in 1937.

Hook Norton was one of the largest villages in Oxfordshire but even with a population of 1,153 in 1931 few people used the railway during the 1920s and 30s. Official statistics for 1935–9 show between 2,996 and 3,199 tickets sold per year, i.e. just 40–64 tickets per week. Parcels were around 40 forwarded and 12 received. Coal received averaged between 26 and 44 tons a week, whilst general merchandise received was between 413 and 531 tons per week, with some 32–75 tons forwarded.

In 1930 station master Frank Owen Coppage had a staff of four – two signalmen, Bill Waring and Jim Fairbrother, and two porters, Walter Hall and Fred Warren.

Frank Coppage lived with his wife and family at The Green, Hook Norton. He was a church warden, chairman of the Hook Norton Football Club, the Pig Club and the Rural District Council. He is remembered with respect by local people and his involvement in local societies was such that some referred to him as 'Mr Hook Norton'. Harold Hall recalls "On Thursdays Mr. Coppage travelled to Banbury on the 12.30 p.m. Kingham to Banbury auto-car to attend a council meeting – we never saw any more of him that day as he was driven back by one of his council colleagues during the evening. He was a very popular and fair man – I remember, for example, when Walter and I were due to play football on Saturday

WESTGATE LIBRARY, OXFORD

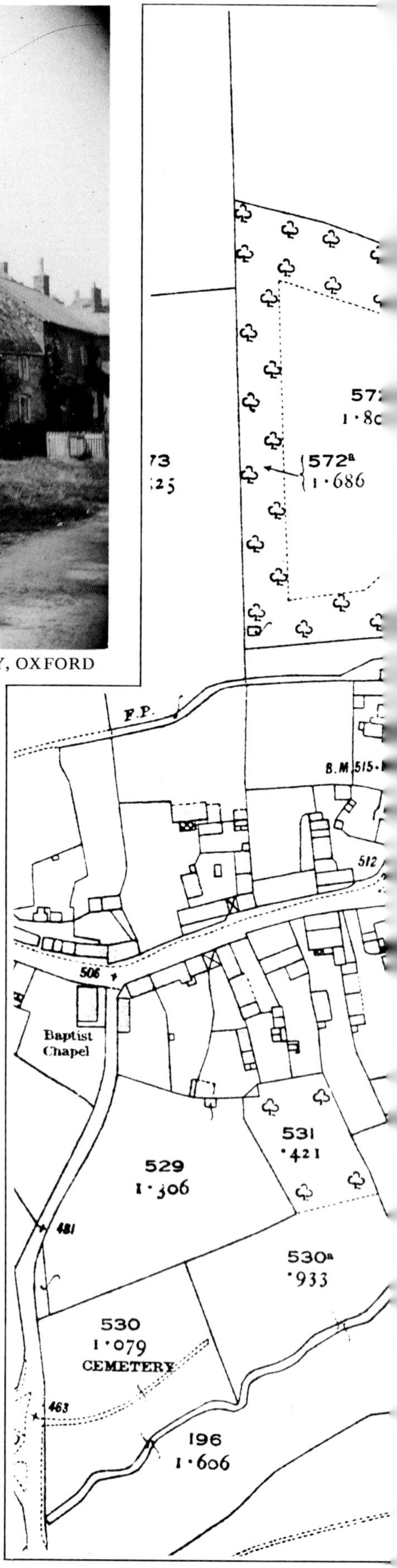

afternoon, he let us slip off and covered the station work himself."

Walter Hall, who came from Bledington, lodged in Hook Norton with the Marshalls at Downend whilst Fred lodged at Mrs. Gulliver's house.

The signalmen worked alternate weekly shifts of 6.0 a.m.–2.0 p.m. and 2.0 p.m.–10.0 p.m. so the early-turn signalman was the first to arrive in the morning and he opened the signal box and the station and booked the passengers for the first train, the 6.22 a.m. auto-car from Banbury, which conveyed daily newspapers for Turnock, the local newsagent, who sent his son John up to collect them. "He had a bike with a large carrier on the front and took the papers back to the shop for sorting." The first of the day's parcels also arrived on this train. Passengers included local women employed at Bliss Mills, Chipping Norton, who were season ticket holders.

The auto returned from Kingham at 7.50 a.m. and, by the time it reached Hook Norton at 8.15, Fred Warren, after walking from his lodgings, had reached the station in time to sign on duty at 8.0 a.m. Frank Coppage also arrived around the same time. While incoming parcels routed via Kingham were being taken off the car for booking in, Brymbo workers Percy Hearn and Frederick Carter got off the train which had brought them in from Chipping Norton. Two or three pupils for Banbury Grammar School then climbed on board – they were also season ticket holders. Harold recalls "I remember one was the son of Roland Newton, our local hay merchant". Other daily travellers to Banbury used the buses which, by this time, were starting to make inroads into rail traffic." "There were more parcels to book off this train."

Fred's predecessor, Harold Hall, had worked at Hook Norton on the opposite shift to his brother. At that time, 1927–9, the porters' shifts were 6.30 a.m.–2.30 p.m. and 1.30 p.m.–9.30 p.m. This earlier start had meant the porter, who entered the station via the side gate (which had already been opened by the signalman), collected the keys from the signal box and unlocked the station rooms. In the winter months he lit the fires and turned up the oil lights, attended the 6.22 a.m. Banbury–Kingham autocar and handed the cash bag to the guard.

After the train had gone, Harold went to the signal box for a fry-up. "I usually took a couple of eggs in with me most days. There were more parcels to book off the 8.15 and, after I'd done this, Mr. Coppage arrived and took over from me in the office."

Besides being booked in, parcels received off the train were supposed to be weighed and stamped before being col-

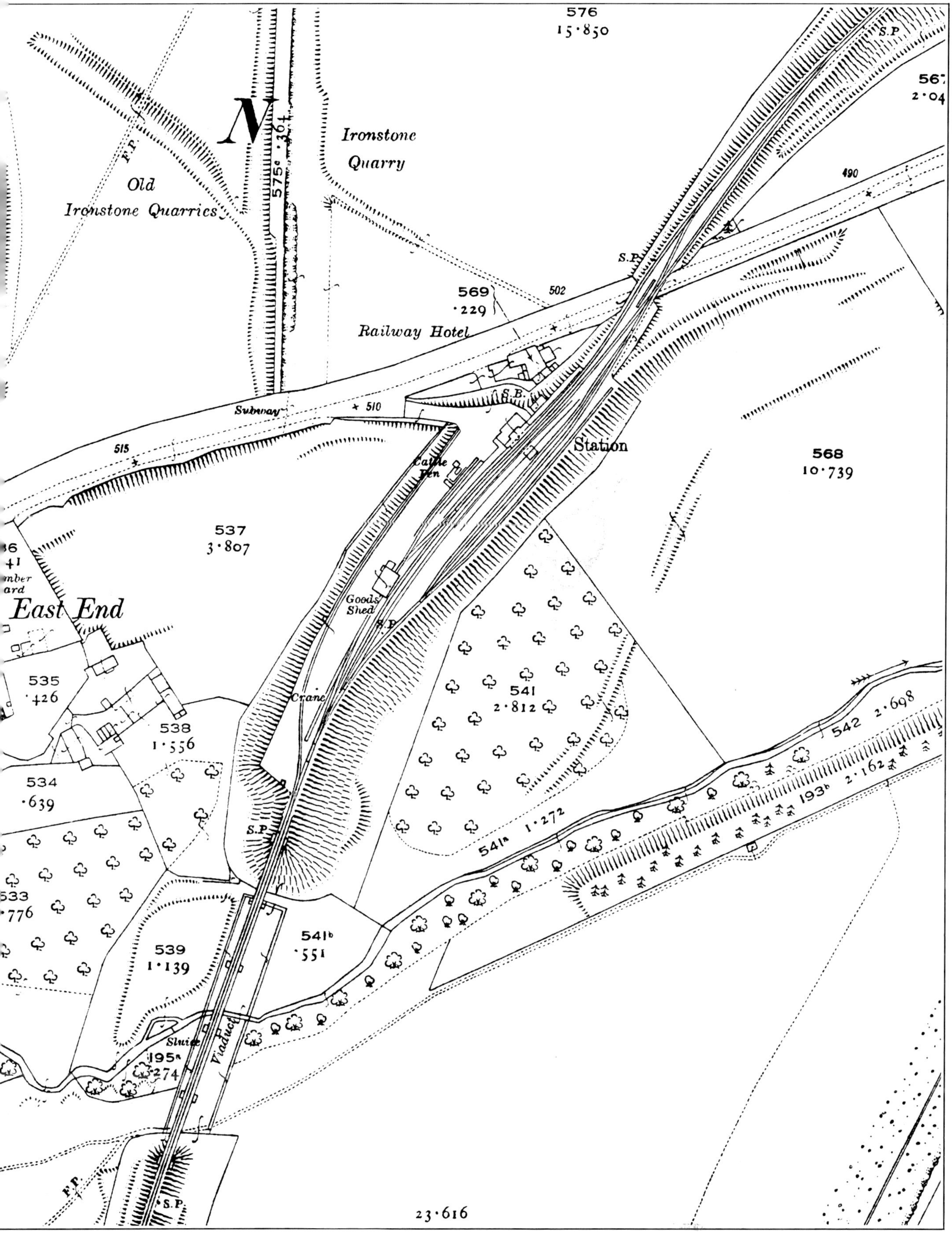

Taken from 25-inch Ordnance Survey for 1922.

This winter shot shows garden trellis adjacent to the down platform waiting room. L&GRP

The down side waiting room in 1947 with the evening sun penetrating the rather stark interior. Those familiar with the dark and light stone colours of GWR stations will easily imagine the beauty of this scene, the red brick, the two-tone livery on the doors and the blue brick paving all being enhanced with the golden light of the sun's rays. J. H. RUSSELL

Another view of the waiting rooms on the same occasion. J. H. RUSSELL

lected or delivered, but Fred recalled "We should have checked all of them but we never did!" In both Harold and Fred's time, the early-turn porter then delivered the parcels around the village – usually between 9.0 and 10.0.

Since Hook Norton was a large village, the station had use of a three-wheeled pedal-driven trolley. Fred described it as "like an ice cream cart", and said that he'd never seen one at any other station. Harold Hall remembers that it "had a brown box on the front with a hinged lid for keeping things dry and there was an open wire tray to hold larger items. It had 'GWR' stamped on the frame – when not in use, we kept it in the waiting room. I've never seen a bike like it before or since." Fred also remembers "It was really a trike and in my time we kept it overnight in the goods shed with the sliding door locked. During the day we kept it handy on the platform. It had a box which opened out at the front and into which items were placed. There was no official collection and delivery service for larger items and to outlying areas – people brought items in themselves or one of the coalmen would do the honours – we sent the usual postcard advice for people to collect items." Fred Warren remembers "in the 1930s Mr. and Mrs. Mobley ran a bus which sometimes called in to deal with a delivery – they also ran the bus to Banbury on Thursday Market days." Pedalling the cart round the meandering lanes of Hook Norton was hard work when it was fully laden. As Harold Hall described it, recalling his time as an early-turn porter in 1928, "You wouldn't take it down the hills because you couldn't get it back up again. So we chained it to whatever we could find and walked round the village." Any parcels received were signed for on a delivery note.

Among the items delivered by the porters were Lyons cakes from London via Banbury for Haynes, the local baker, and perishable items which had arrived in the roadside truck from Hockley on the previous day's down goods. Clothing was delivered to Hicks, the drapers, ironmongery to Turnock's store in High Street (who also sold petrol and tools), and chocolates and confectionery to Pilsworth's grocers. "Quite a bit of stuff also came in for Miles, the tobacconist."

Items of postage would be delivered to the Post Office, which in the 1920s was kept by Tom Cox and afterwards by Heath. Tom Cox was also a stonemason employed at Brymbo works.

In the early 1920s postage items were specifically delivered by out-porter Joe Randle, who also collected the mail from the Post Office to meet the 12.50 and 5.0 p.m. trains which took it to head office in Banbury. It is possible that by the late 1920s the out-porter's position was combined with the general porters' duties.

Fred would take the lamps out of the signals and dummy signals and brought them in for the signalman to trim and refuel them ready for him to take back out. The outer home signal was located between the two viaducts and the porters had to cross the 188 yard long Viaduct No. 1 to reach it. This was not always a pleasant experience, as Harold Hall put it, "Bit breezy over the 'ducts". Fred remembered just how windy it could get on the viaducts, recalling that there wasn't a safe place one could get to if a train was coming.

In Harold's time, the early-turn porter finished his 6.30–2.30 shift with cleaning duties, covering the booking office as required. "We also assisted with the shunting and yard work, any heavy work such as sheeting being dealt with when we [the early and late-turn porters] were both on during the overlap period of our shifts [late shift 1.30–9.30]. Incidentally, we also dealt with the parcels accounts which had to be scrutinised by Mr. Coppage." The signalmen dealt similarly with the goods accounts for which they received an enhancement to their pay.

When Harold was on early shift, his brother Walter called in at his lodgings to collect Harold's lunch. "Mrs. Marshall used to wrap the plate up and put it in a basket." When he was on lates, he had lunch before he set off.

In Fred's time, the late-turn porter's shift was 12.0–8.0 p.m. with an hour out for tea, but Walter Hall frequently arrived between 11.0 and 11.30 a.m. With his 8.0 a.m. start, Fred took an hour out for lunch, often walking back to his lodgings for the break. However, if the weather persuaded him to stay at the station, he ate his lunch in the weighbridge office, light-

As mentioned in Vol. 1, this GWR signal box was a replacement for the original Gloucester Wagon Co. cabin situated on the down platform. Classified as a Type 27C by the Signalling Record Society, it was opened on 8th December 1907 and housed a 33-lever 5.2in stud frame, the locking room dimensions being officially recorded as 25ft x 12ft with a height of 7ft to the operating floor.
J. H. MOSS

This 1930s staff group, taken outside the signal box, shows signalman Walter Hall (second from left) and ganger Tom Wyatt (third from left). The other figures, a guard and perhaps a porter, have yet to be identified.
CTY. J. H. VENN

The north-east elevation of the signal box c.1952-3. Notice how the gracefully curved end of the canopy valancing on the station building had been cut away to ease sighting difficulties following the newly positioned replacement signal box. J. H. MOSS

54XX 0–6–0PT No. 5404 alongside the up platform with an autocar for Banbury. Locos were generally coupled to the Kingham end of the auto-trailers so that they were hauled on the outward journey and, as seen here, propelled on the return. W. A. CAMWELL

ing the fire to keep warm. As Fred recalled, "Nobody else lit the fire in there".

The down goods was scheduled to call between 12.40 and 2.0 p.m. but the time was variable, depending upon the quantity of goods traffic involved, but both porters were usually available to deal with it. After arriving on the down loop, the Hook Norton wagons, which often included a station truck next to the engine, were detached and set back into the yard where they were kept 'on the engine' while the outwards wagons were collected for return to Banbury.

The station truck or 'roadside wagon' was put into the goods shed for unloading. It was used for specialised goods, non-perishables and any items too big to be conveyed by passenger train. Harold recalls "the truck came from the Oxford area and I think it returned to Hockley – we didn't get a lot of traffic, the most

Views around goods yards are not very easily come by but this photo of the end loading dock behind the up platform provides a glimpse of the cattle pens, the timber-built office of the South Wales and Cannock Chase Coal Company and the roof of the Railway Inn. J. H. MOSS

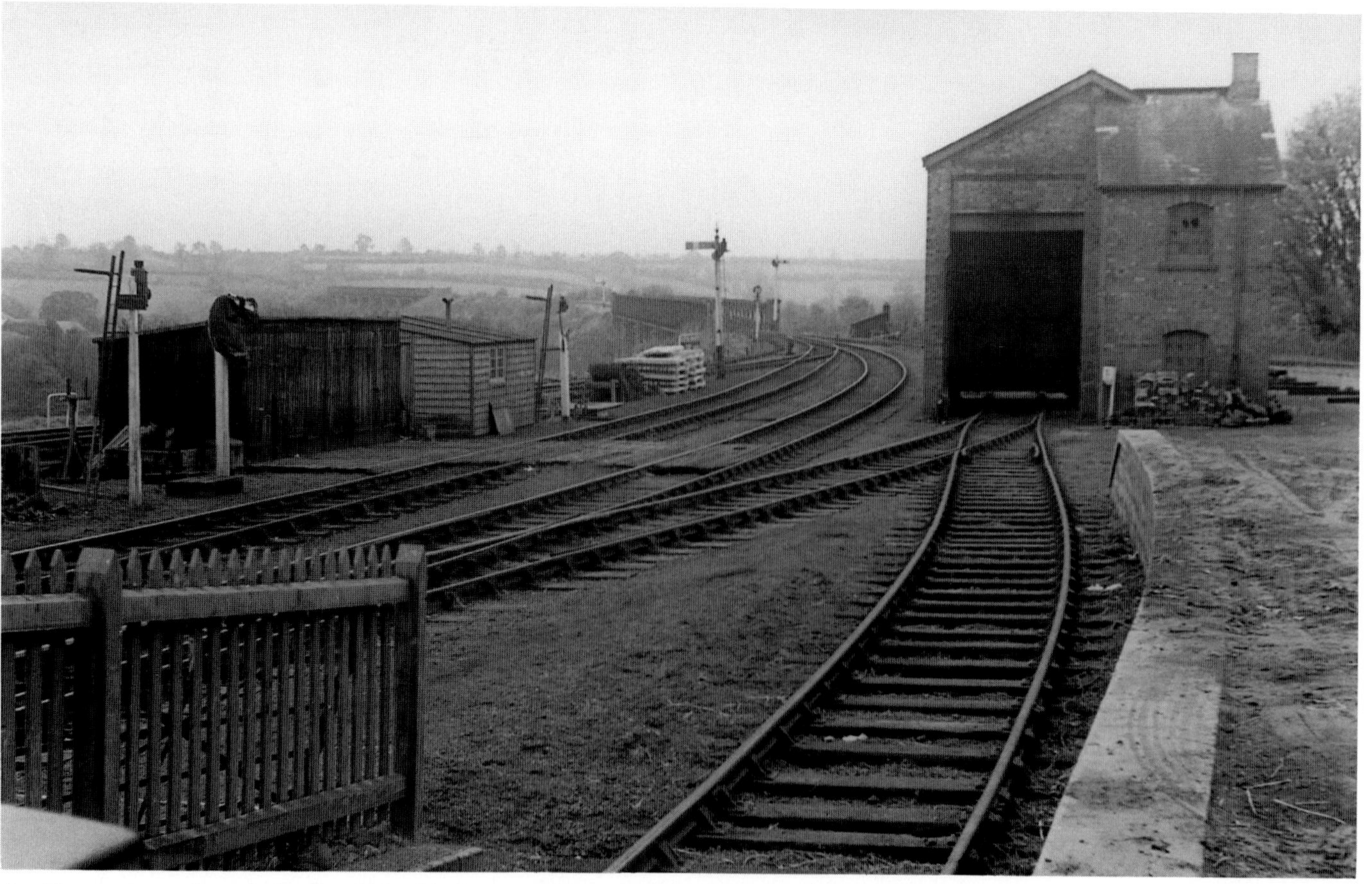

Looking south-east from the loading dock with the two viaducts carrying the line across the valley towards the tunnel at South Hill. The sheds on the left behind the single-line staff apparatus housed the gangers' motorised trolleys whilst the adjacent shed with the window was the PW cabin. The Hook Norton permanent way gang had been responsible for the length from midway between Rollright and Hook Norton to Wiggington until c.1930 when it was amalgamated with the Bloxham gang under the Economic System of Maintenance. The length then ran from midway between Rollright and Hook Norton to between Milton and Adderbury. The gang signed on at 7.0 a.m. at Hook Norton. J. H. RUSSELL

As already explained, the red brick goods shed was one of three built to the same design on this section of the Banbury & Cheltenham Direct Railway. As with the others, the loading deck inside was equipped with a 1½-ton crane. J. H. MOSS

GOODS TRAFFIC

OUTWARDS

Hay – Roland Newton was a local hay merchant who lived near Hook Norton Brewery. He purchased supplies from local farms having checked that their hay was suitable for purchase. He employed bailers who were very skilled men and supplies were brought to the station on a horse-drawn trailer or by hauliers' lorries for despatch. "They used to load on the back road and we kept our eye on them to see there was no overloading. The hay was loaded flat with two or three bales over the top which cleared the gauge."

William Slatter, the agent for the South Wales and Cannock Chase Coal Company, helped load it onto the railway wagons. The sheeting was carried out when the two porters were on duty between 1.30 and 2.30 p.m. Porter Harold Hall recalls, "It was a two-man job – I preferred to carry a sheet over my shoulder when climbing up on the wagon. Newton specified three sheets for his loads – the first was laid across centrally and the others overlapped at each end. The ropes were taken diagonally from one headstock to the other. We used to have about 100 bales to each wagon – a lorry load usually equalled a wagon load." At the peak of the season, up to two trucks were despatched to a variety of destinations, some being sold to the GWR.

This prefabricated traders store was probably added following a July 1950 works order which authorised the provision of storage accommodation for Messrs. J. Bibby & Son.
COLLECTION ALAN BRAIN

Straw – Straw was also loaded in the back road and dealt with by the Banbury-based firm of B. T. Frost. "It was collected up and brought to the station by Frost's men, who loaded it into the wagons. After the first layer across the floor, they stood bales up at both ends of the wagon to stop the load moving around – this was done because, being very compressed, it could move about easily." Harold Hall said "When we sheeted and roped, we took the rope right around the wagon in addition to across – in a similar way to securing hay. We overlapped the sheets and if, for example, the wagon was going north from Banbury, we made the overlap so the sheets would not rise in the direction of travel."

Hops – Incoming goods included irregular supplies of hops and sugar for Hook Norton Brewery, who used a horse-drawn dray to collect them from the goods shed loading dock. Fred Warren recalled that it was the only time he remembered the goods shed rear doors being open.

Sugar beet – Sugar beet was brought to the station during the season by local farmers who loaded into open wagons and sent it to the sugar refinery at Kidderminster.

INWARDS

Coal – Most supplies were received from Coventry and routed via Banbury, Binley and Baddesley being two collieries remembered. The merchants were:

South Wales and Cannock Chase Co. leased wharfage in the goods yard "near the crane" and had a hut near the weighbridge. It was constructed of timber and contained a desk, seat and stove. In the 1920s and 30s their agent was William Slatter. Tom Powell recalls when his father, Thomas Hollier Powell, farmed at Home Farm in Wigginton in the 1920s, he collected coal from Hook Norton station using a horse-drawn wagon. A six or seven-ton wagon load would last up to six months.

"They usually had two or three wagons in each week on the back road, opposite to their coal office, and some of their supplies were also kept at their wharf at the neck of the goods yard, near the crane. Fred Warren recalled two or three wagons of coal a week arriving in the company's own wagons. They were black with white lettering "which covered virtually the whole of their sides." William Slatter owned a lorry which he used to deliver coal around the village.

Williams – "He only usually had a truck each month – he lived round the corner from the station."

Welford – This Oxford-based firm received about two or three wagons each week. Like South Wales and Cannock Chase, they had their own wagons which are remembered as black with white lettering.

This view, taken on 2nd June 1951, gives the passengers' view from the centre door of a Diagram U auto-trailer being propelled into Hook Norton station on the 12.45 p.m. Kingham to Banbury service. Although the permanent way materials had cluttered the site, this picture nevertheless provides a view of the ironstone sidings behind the down platform. J. E. NORRIS

regular being cloth for Hicks, the local draper". All roadside goods were signed for. Any heavy small parcels which the porters didn't want to transfer to the booking office were locked up in the goods office attached to the goods shed. Any items destined for Banbury and beyond went back with the station truck on the return journey from Kingham. Not long after the goods arrived, shunting was interrupted for the passage of the 12.30 p.m. Kingham to Banbury auto, which arrived at 12.56 p.m. The outgoing or 'Banbury' wagons were put on the shed road where they were left for collection on the return journey whilst inwards wagons were put on the back road, and after the shunting was completed the goods shed doors were closed across the rails.

The porters also helped with the ironstone trains for the nearby Brymbo Ironstone Company's works at Council Hill. As already explained, the sidings there could only be served by up trains so all empty wagons were taken into Hook Norton station where they were put into the sidings behind the down platform, run round and taken back to Council Hill, or Brymbo as it was more commonly known.

The output from these workings was considerably greater than that at Adderbury and Bloxham, the traffic being included in the 'other minerals forwarded' figures for Hook Norton station. They ranged from 41,922 tons in 1935 and 83,441 in 1937 to wartime output of 100,266 in 1940 and 161,602 in 1943.

When Archie Warren worked as a porter there in 1939 he remembers the ironstone train leaving Banbury at 2.5 p.m. The Winter 1938/9 Service Timetable shows a 12.43 p.m. Banbury to Hook Norton train returning at 2.5 p.m. on Tuesdays, Thursdays and Saturdays but this is not remembered by staff. "After arrival at Hooky with the empties, we set back onto the wagons already in one of the loops, cut off the brake and shunted the fresh wagons to the other loop or siding alongside ready for the next day. We then ran round and took what was a new set of empties to Brymbo, returning from Hook Norton at 4.40 p.m. If more wagons were needed, we collected them from the other loop and attached them to the front of our train. The late-turn porter rode out to Brymbo sidings to assist with shunting there and walked back after the train had left the sidings for Banbury.

In the late 1920s, the empties which left Banbury at 4.27 p.m. were simply run round at Hook Norton where they arrived in the up platform and, after the departure of the 5.5 p.m. Kingham to Banbury car, were drawn forward for the brake van to be detached at the west end of the platform. The wagons were then drawn further forward clear of the trailing points and backed into one of the loop sidings behind the down platform. Then, after collecting the brake van and attaching it to what would now be the rear of the train, the engine was run to the opposite end of the formation, via the up platform and the trailing connection over the road bridge, and coupled onto the train ready for departure back to the Ironstone Sidings at 6.5 p.m. – again with the Hook Norton late-turn porter accompanying the guard.

When Banbury was congested, empty iron ore wagons were brought out on the

Churchward 2–6–0 No. 5379 at Hook Norton with a Banbury to Kingham goods. Hook Norton was the mid-point of the journey and the place where the goods crew stopped for lunch. The Banbury enginemen were noted for the meticulous care they gave to their locomotives.
COLLECTION ALAN BRAIN

Lengthening shadows indicate that this panoramic view of the station from the up home signal was taken on a sunny evening during the spring of 1947. It shows the pointwork at the neck of the yard and makes an interesting comparison with the view on page 145 of Vol. 1. The coal behind the sleeper-built PW cabin was being stored by the South Wales and Cannock Chase Coal Company. As mentioned in the history, the back siding on the left was a later addition. There was no yard crane here. J. H. RUSSELL

The view from the deck of the No. 1 viaduct. The regulations for Hook Norton stated that trains should be brought under control before crossing viaducts in order to avoid applying the brakes while on them. However, shunting the yard unavoidably involved running backwards and forwards onto the first viaduct and braking on it. Fireman Michael Clifton recalls that when they came to a stand during movements in and out of the yard, the crew could feel the steelwork quivering beneath the engine, whilst on the move they could also experience singing of the steelwork.

J. H. RUSSELL

Looking south-east from the station with, in the distance, an approaching Kingham to Banbury autocar on the embankment between the two viaducts in 1951. The Iron Mink vans stabled on a panel of unconnected track were stationed there to provide additional warehousing. One of these is evident close to the new warehouse in the picture on page 293. On 14th March 1941 the catchpoints at the end of the ironstone sidings on the left were run through by an engine working one of the ironstone trains for Brymbo. The accident report read as follows: 'The 2.5 p.m. Freight, Banbury to Hook Norton, arrived at the latter point at 4.16 p.m. and was immediately shunted into the sidings. Apparently there was some misunderstanding between the Signalman and Trainmen in regard to whether or not it would be possible for the engine to run round the train before it was necessary to clear the line for the acceptance of the 3.50 p.m. Auto Car ex Banbury. As a result the engine moved forward after the Signalman had reversed the points, i.e. with the disc in the 'on' position, and in consequence the engine (G.W. 3048) was derailed at the catchpoint all tender wheels and two pairs of driving wheels. The running line was not fouled and the working of other trains was not interfered with. The Banbury breakdown vans were requisitioned, arriving 5.35 p.m. and the rerailing of the engine was completed at 11.40 p.m., having been somewhat delayed through blackout conditions and an air raid 'alert'.'
W. A. CAMWELL

daily goods train and stored in the down siding, alongside the loops behind the down platform. When this happened, the ore wagons were detached before the yard work began.

Apart from the shunting, Fred's duties in the afternoon were primarily to meet the 4.5 p.m. auto from Banbury and deal with the traffic originating from the pick-up goods, wash down the platforms, trim the wicks in the station lamps, clean all the spare lamps, which was carried out in the weighbridge office, and fill the tank in the lavatories with water from the pump. He finished at 5.0 p.m. The late-turn porter's duty, worked by Walter Hall, lasted until 9.30 so he would have helped with the return pick-up goods and met the 5.20 p.m auto from Kingham, the 7.40 p.m. from Banbury and the return working from Kingham at 8.55 p.m. When the up goods arrived, it stopped short of the trailing crossover at the foot of the up platform where the engine was uncoupled, run forward and then back into the goods shed to pick up the station truck, which was then propelled out through the other end of the building to collect the 'Banbury' wagons left there earlier. These vehicles were then taken into the platform and backed onto the rest of the train ready for departure. During this time the 7.40 p.m. auto-car from Banbury called on its way to Kingham. Certainly it was not unusual for Walter to remain on duty until 10.0 or even 11.0 p.m. in order, for example, to help with loading wagons of hay for Roland Newton.

Occasionally, horse-boxes and cattle wagons were conveyed on the rear of passenger trains. If a wagon arrived from Kingham, it was set back towards the goods shed, from where it was pinch-barred into the dock. If one arrived from the Banbury direction, the train drew clear of the yard and set back to the shed road, from where the box was positioned in the same way. Harold recalled "We used to get cattle, mainly via Banbury, on the late afternoon train." In 1929, 113 wagons were handled but traffic then showed a dramatic fall and by 1939 only eleven wagons were recorded.

THE VIADUCT, HOOK NORTON

The five-span northernmost No. 1 viaduct, viewed looking north-west. The inset stone panels in the abutment parapets were recessed on this viaduct, whereas on the larger No. 2 viaduct, they were raised. M. QUARTERMAIN

J. H. RUSSELL

Panoramic view of the eight-span No. 2 viaduct from South Hill. COLLECTION A. BRAIN

The lane passing between the village and Park Farm was carried beneath the first span of the No. 2 viaduct. Local schoolchildren would run to the viaducts to see the trains passing overhead. Paul Eagles recalled that the steelwork "used to shake like anything".

NATIONAL RAILWAY MUSEUM and J. H. RUSSELL

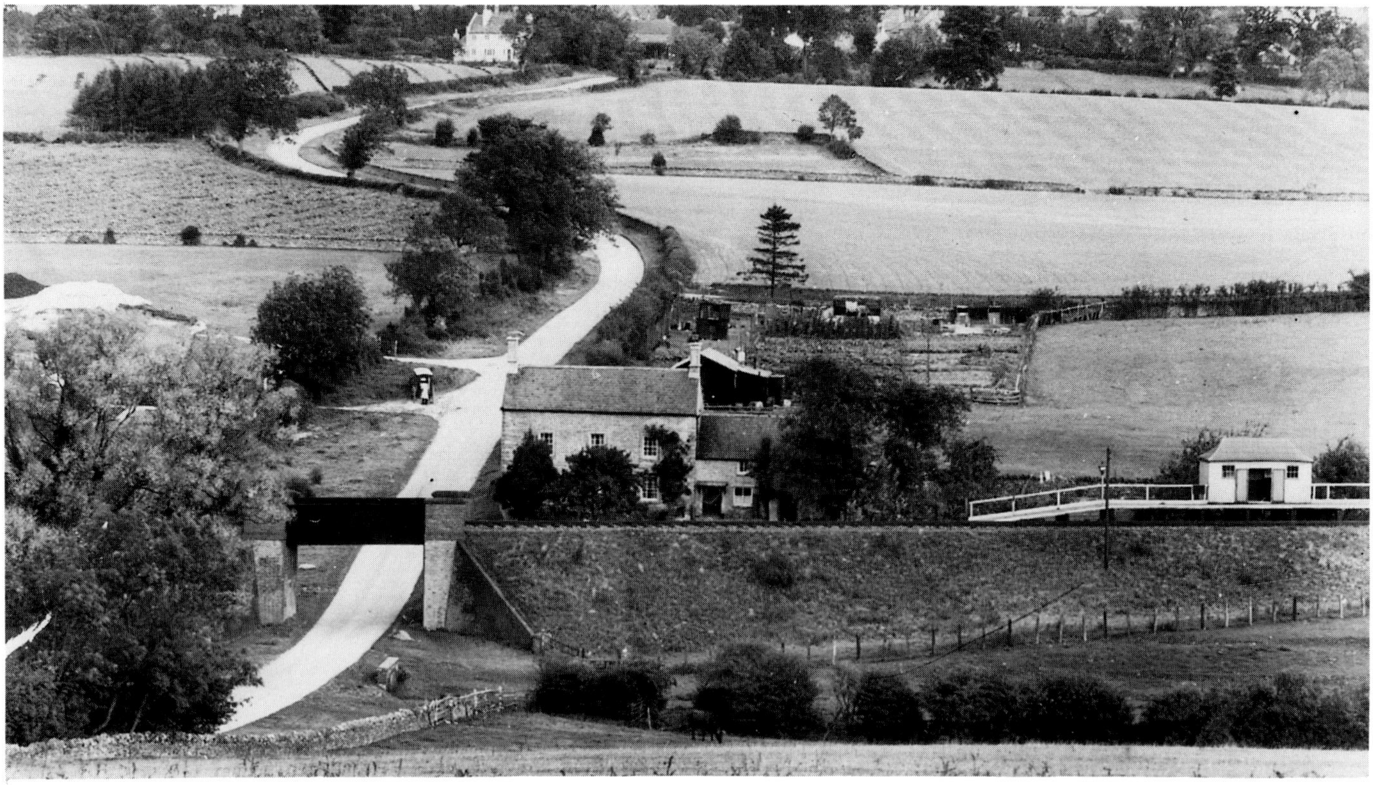

Lime Kiln House overlooking the halt was named after the nearby Lime Kiln Quarry which dated from at least as long ago as 1774. It was still producing quicklime for mortar in the 1920s and possibly even into the early 1930s. Sylvia Harris recalls that in the 1940s, when she held a season ticket from Rollright to Chipping Norton, she and the other girls who worked at the Bliss Mill could often see the train passing over the bridge as they walked down the hill towards the halt and that the engine driver would reverse his train back to collect them. F. R. PACKER

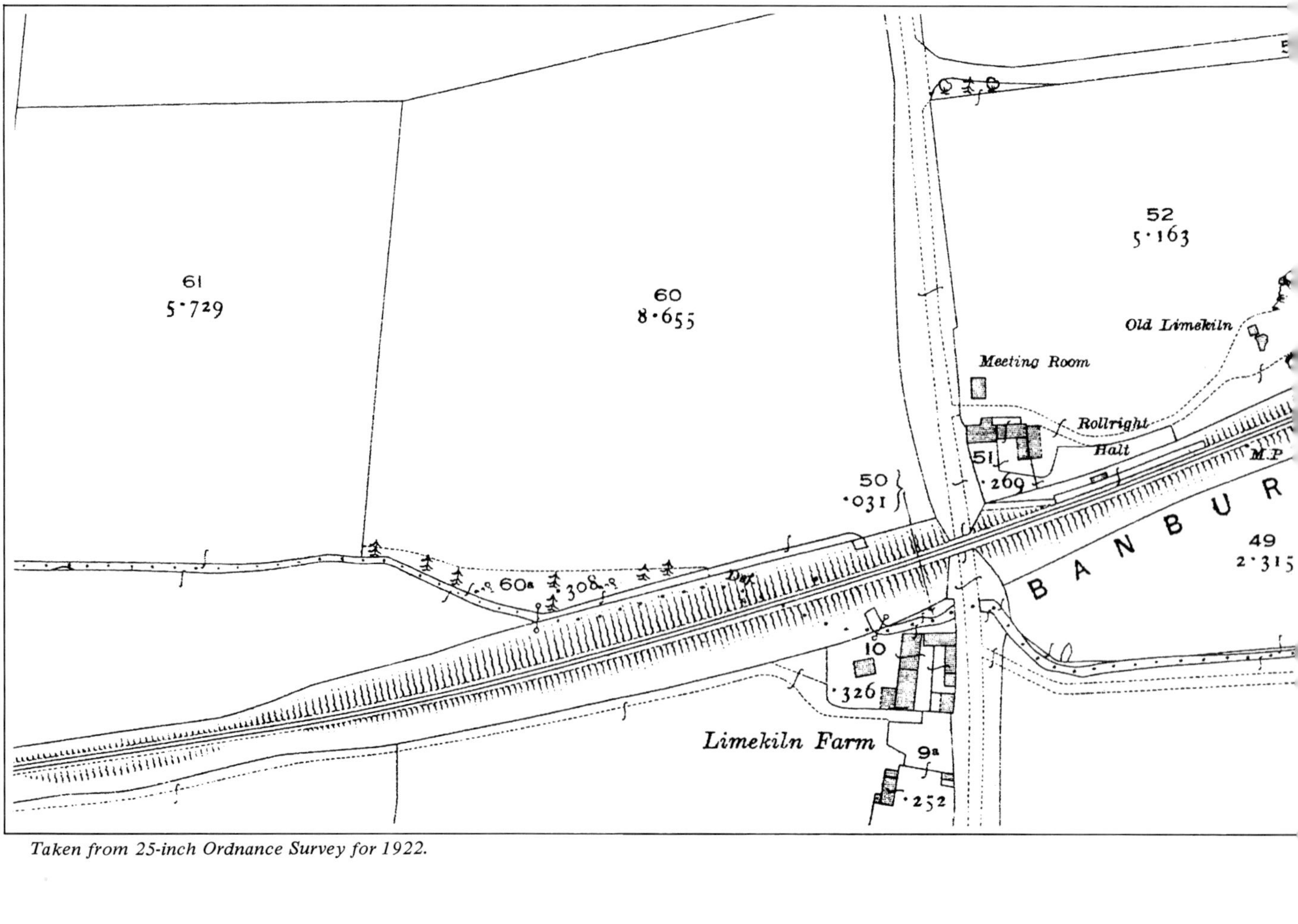

Taken from 25-inch Ordnance Survey for 1922.

ROLLRIGHT HALT 95m 2c

ROLLRIGHT Halt was a late arrival on the scene, opening on 12th December 1906 after many years of campaigning by the inhabitants of the nearby village of Great Rollright. The goods siding, located 200 yds east of the halt, was not opened until March 1909. Unfortunately for our purpose, the official statistics of traffic at Rollright Halt were again, as with Milton Halt, included with the figures for Banbury. Therefore, we are solely dependent on the recollections of surviving staff for the level of activity there.

Since at least 1922 and up to the mid-1940s, the Rollright porter was Joe Harris. He was born around 1875 and lived at Rose Cottage in the nearby village of Great Rollright with his wife, sons Fred and Sydney and daughter Millie. He is believed to have served at Alvescot station on the Fairford branch, then Charlbury, where he met his wife, before taking the post at Rollright.

Joe was a Grade 1 porter working from 9.0 a.m. to 5.0 p.m. Eileen Beacham, a Rollright girl, who went on to marry Banbury engineman Bill Green, recalled Joe "leaving home with his box or bag and wearing his peaked hat, to go to the little office at the halt."

Porter Harold Hall remembers him with affection. "He got all the rabbits for all the guards that came on the train and Joe always had a couple of rabbits spare . . . you could always get a rabbit off Joe."

Harold Hall covered the duty for a period during the 1930s, relieving for Joe Harris while he was away on holiday. He recalls that "most of our passengers were women who worked at Bliss Mill in 'Chippy'. As there was nobody to book them in the morning, they arranged to get their season tickets at 'Chippy'. Other passengers were mainly shoppers going to Chipping Norton. I can't honestly remember booking any passengers. A Mr.

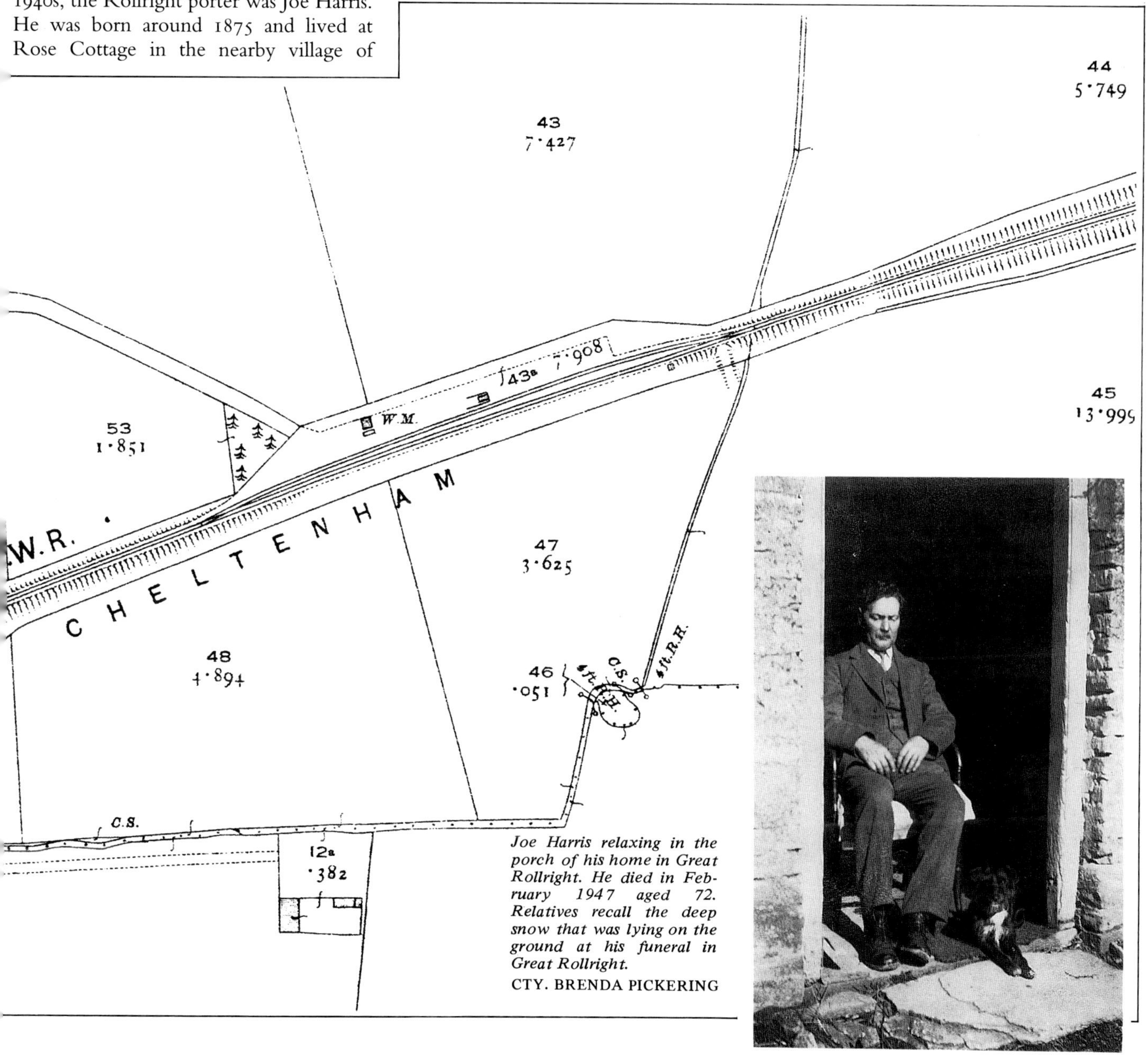

Joe Harris relaxing in the porch of his home in Great Rollright. He died in February 1947 aged 72. Relatives recall the deep snow that was lying on the ground at his funeral in Great Rollright.

CTY. BRENDA PICKERING

Harvey, a local pheasant breeder, sent birds and eggs away – they went all over. It was a lonely place – most days you only spoke to the coal merchant and the permanent way staff. Other traffic was very small and there was evidently an arrangement whereby parcels could be left and collected from a small hut in the station approach."

Fred Warren also relieved at Rollright (among many other stations) after being laid off from his porter's post at Hook Norton. He took the train from Kingham to Rollright at 8.0 a.m., porter George Smith handing him the Rollright keys on his way through Chipping Norton and Fred returning them at the end of the week.

The main traffic at the siding was coal, the local merchant James Taplin living in the large house, Lime Kiln House, to the north of the halt. He rented 60 sq yds wharfage in the yard and delivered supplies by lorry.

Another coal merchant, Nash's of Long Compton, also received supplies there because it was "nearer than the coal depot at Shipston on Stour".

The eastern approach to the halt, down the gentle 1 in 700 gradient, seen here from one of the loading banks on a winter's day in 1950 with the covered east end ground frame which was locked by a key on the single-line staff. J. H. RUSSELL

Sugar beet was regularly despatched for many years by Mr. Wishart, a Scottish farmer who was tenant at Manor Farm, on behalf of the farm manager Mr. Frazer. When he loaded it into railway wagons at the siding, Eileen Green recalls "the tractor and cart always left a trail of mud on the road."

Both ends of the siding were connected to the running line by means of points worked from adjacent ground frames locked by a key incorporated in the end of the single-line train staff.

In the late 1930s, the only traffic recalled was coal which arrived on the pick-up goods which called between 2.11 and 2.40 p.m. The train pulled up short of the westernmost connection to the siding where the wagons for Rollright were uncoupled, then drawn forward clear of the points. The driver handed the single-line train staff to the guard who inserted it in the ground frame to unlock the levers in order to operate the points. The engine then backed into the siding, picked up any outgoing wagons and ran back out again to put them on the waiting train, before returning to the siding with the incoming traffic.

When outgoing wagons were not picked up on the down journey, the empties were pushed to the eastern end of the loop for collection on the return journey, but as the number of wagons was usually insignificant and there was no one on duty at the siding when the train was on its way back to Banbury, Harold says, "We made it the practice to clear the empties via 'Chippy', so the pick-up didn't need to call on its way back." At Chipping Norton, the outgoing Rollright wagons were simply added to the Chipping Norton wagons awaiting collection. Peter Scarsbrook covered the porter's duties in 1943, also assisting at Chipping Norton. He worked alongside Joe Harris, who by that time was approaching the end of his career. He recalls Joe as "a really old stager, always taking snuff... he had this snuff box and all the way down the front of his waistcoat was stained with brown snuff powder." He worked almost to the end of his life and died in the cold winter of 1947, aged 72.

After Joe Harris retired, Charlie Cranmer took over the porter's duties at Rollright and remained there through the British Railways years.

An earlier view east during the summer of 1947 with the platelayers hut on the right and a standard GWR loading gauge with railbuilt post.
J. H. RUSSELL

The corrugated-iron goods shed where goods could be locked awaiting collection or despatch. J. H. RUSSELL

This 1947 view shows most of the siding with its brick-built weighbridge office, the 60 sq yds of James Taplin's coal wharf, the wooden post of the original 1908 loading gauge, the platform-mounted goods shed (behind the wagons) and the sleeper-walled loading bank at the far end. J. H. RUSSELL

The south elevation of the corrugated-iron goods shed. J. H. RUSSELL

The side and rear elevations of the brick office. Inside were block repeater bells to indicate a train entering the section. J. H. RUSSELL

Looking east in 1947, with the covered ground frame, which controlled entry to the siding at the west end of the layout, in the foreground. J. H. RUSSELL

The Ports-to-Ports express approaching Rollright Halt in August 1932. The platform originally extended almost to the road bridge, but was shortened, probably around the period of the First World War.
COLLECTION ALAN BRAIN

As this view of Rollright Halt in 1947 includes a glimpse of the siding, it provides an idea of the proximity of the two parts of the establishment. The line at this point was falling at 1 in 112 towards Chipping Norton. Former engineman Doug Cunningham recalls: "If there was nobody at the halts and nobody wanted to get off, we didn't stop." A small fire at the halt in 1940 is recorded in an official report: 'At approximately 1.30 p.m. on June 27th the Porter at Great Rollright Sidings observed smoke issuing from the Waiting Shed on Rollright Halt platform. The Porter proceeded to the site and found the floor boards on fire at the entrance to the shed. The engine of the 10.40 a.m. freight, Banbury to Kingham, (which train was standing at Great Rollright Sidings), was detached and taken forward to the Halt where it was utilised to extinguish the conflagration. It is thought the fire may have been caused by a lighted cigarette end, discarded by a passenger, which fell between the floor boards on to a bird's nest which had been built on a joist beneath. The Waiting Shed has been locked pending repairs by the Engineering Department.' In the early 1940s Eileen Beecham, her friend Sylvia and Sylvia's sister caught the train here each morning to Chipping Norton where they worked at Bliss Tweed Mill. They used to chat to the railwaymen and when Eileen was courting fireman Bill Green, who she later married, his driver Tommy Oxlade used to let her ride back home to Rollright on the footplate at night.
J. H. RUSSELL

A 48XX Collett 0–4–2T propelling its single auto-trailer towards the tunnel on its way out of Chipping Norton. C. R. L. COLES

CHIPPING NORTON

97m 75c via King's Sutton 89m 21c via Kingham

EVEN though Chipping Norton was the principal station on the line, by the late 1930s the number of passengers using the railway was disappointing, tickets issued only amounting to between 123 and 136 per week. Parcels averaged 64–74 forwarded each week and 360–392 received. Some 324–374 tons of coal and 106–110 tons of general merchandise were received each week and a mere 16–19 tons were forwarded, whilst 8–11 tons of 'other minerals' were forwarded and 36–76 tons received. The incoming 'other minerals' was probably stone traffic for local road improvements.

When Archie Warren started at Chipping Norton as a lad porter in the late 1930s, the station master was William Williams who lived in The Leys. Madge Tustian was the booking clerk, Fred Darke the goods clerk and Percy Hiatt a regular relief clerk. Uniformed grades included signalmen Ben Collins and Fred Jones on alternate shifts, and porters Charlie Parsons and George Smith. "George suffered from ulcers and needed his meals at regular times so he and Charlie (who had been at the station since 1906) came to an arrangement and George was always on earlies."

Staff based in the goods yard were checker Charlie Hall and lad porter Archie Warren, both on day turns. George Smith is believed to have booked on duty at about 6.45 each morning having walked from his home in The Leys via the foot crossing which led from there to the common. On dark winter mornings he turned on the gas lamps either side of the crossing, then made his way to the station, opening up and turning on the lights ready to deal with the 6.22 a.m. autocar from Banbury which brought in several women workers for Bliss's Mill. This train was also used by regular business travellers who changed to a London-bound train at Kingham and, during the school term, pupils for Milham Ford School at Oxford.

Archie Warren officially worked from 8.0 a.m. to 5.0 p.m. although he was allowed to vary his booking on and off times slightly so that he could travel to and from work on the autocar service, very much like his predecessor Fred Warren.

Archie lived at Bledington with his parents and cycled to Kingham station, where he left his bike under the footbridge stairs on the down side and caught the 7.47 a.m. Banbury train – "the Chippy Dick". On arrival at Chipping Norton, where the train was met by George Smith or even the station master, Archie unloaded parcels from the brake van – "I made a point of checking the parcels at Kingham so I knew what was on board for Chippy. We either manhandled the parcels over

Chipping Norton station, looking towards the tunnel. J. H. MOSS

COLLECTION ALAN BRAIN

the barrow crossing or got a trolley – it all depended on their size and bulk. After the train had gone, the consignments were taken to the parcels office where they were left to be dealt with by the clerk and porter."

Archie booked on in the office, then made his way to the weighbridge hut and, after sweeping the deck, checked the scales, a daily ritual which he recorded in a book. "The yard gates were open by this time – I assume by the early-turn porter – and there were usually coalmen about who wanted loads weighed. Most of this traffic was handled by the Co-op who received around three or four wagons each day, and for their own convenience the coalmen loaded up five bags at 1cwt each and, after weighing the lorry empty, did the same later with bags on. They did it in small amounts like this so they could check their accuracy as they went along. If they needed more coal, they could shovel up some from around the yard to compensate and, having got the first lot right, did another five bags, and so on. It meant using a hell of a lot of weighing tickets. Incidentally, I remember the tickets were in strip form, very much like cloakroom tickets, coloured buff with a carbon and the top copy, which was issued, was perforated. If I remember rightly, the charge was something like tuppence for each ton – the regular users had this added to their account. We recorded the 'tare as weighed' and 'tare as stated'." Lorries and vans due to be taxed were often weighed on the bridge; all extraneous materials affecting their weight being removed, even dirt and grime – "they were often spotless when they came in the yard."

Archie carried on weighing duties until about 9.0, when he went to the goods shed to assist Charlie Hall unload and segregate traffic on the shed deck. Most of the shed traffic arrived on the 9.0 a.m. mixed train from Kingham, which

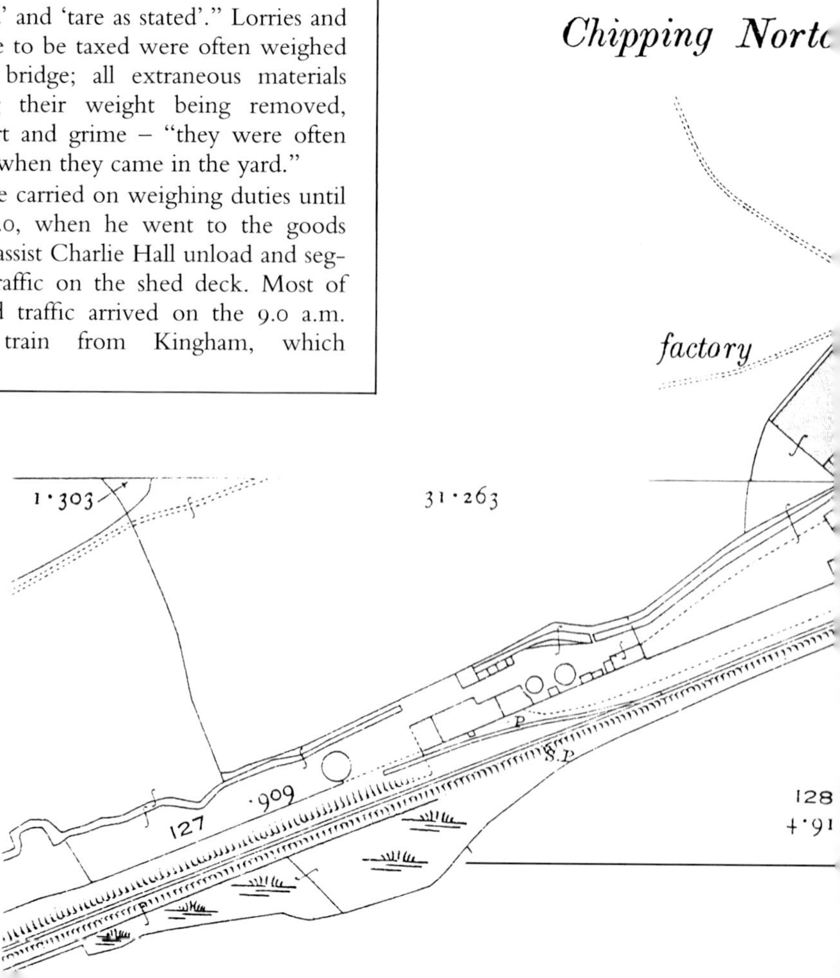

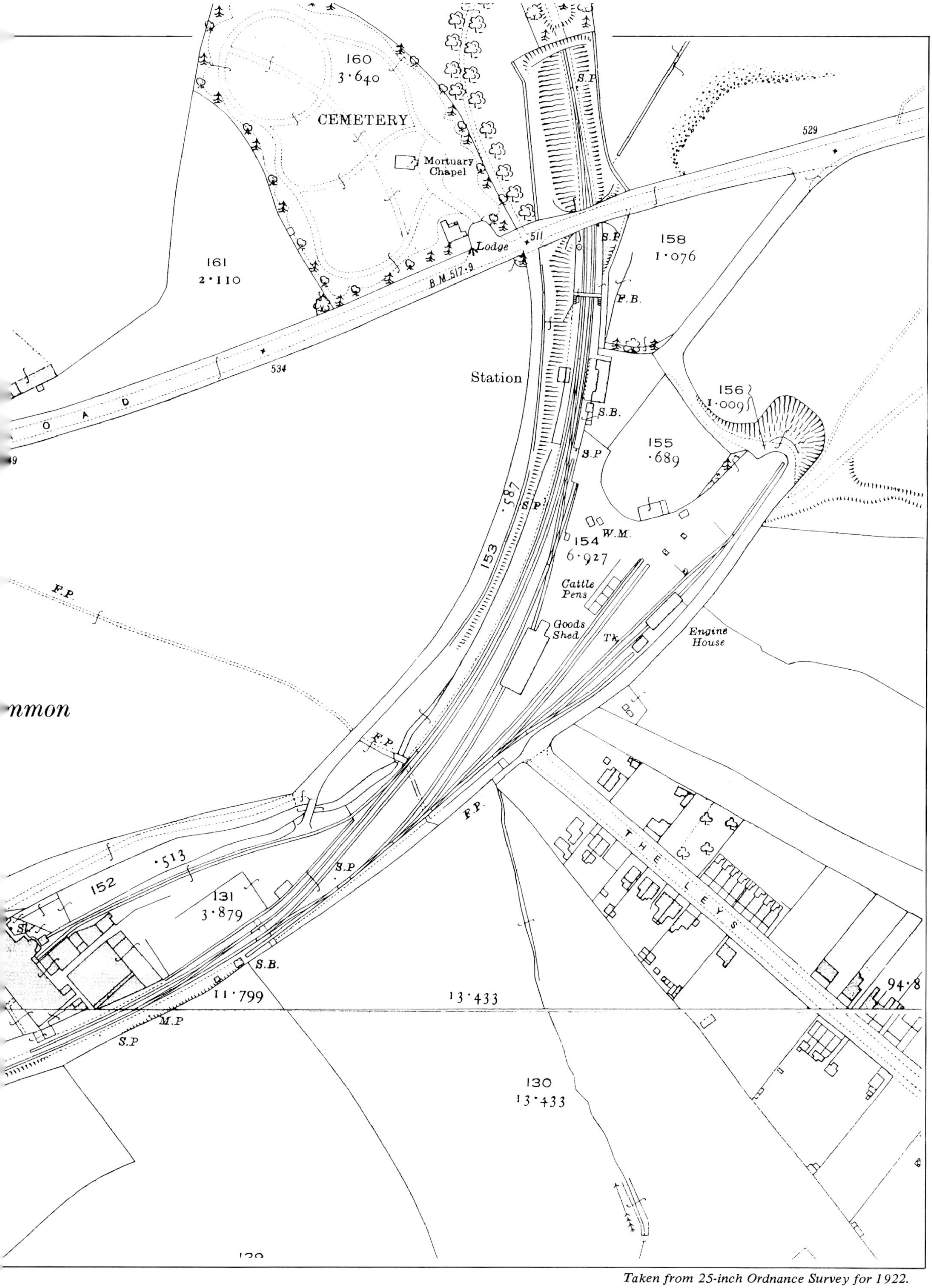

Taken from 25-inch Ordnance Survey for 1922.

Chipping Norton High Street in the 1930s.
AUTHOR'S COLLECTION

The blue-brick portal of the tunnel. The gradient from Chipping Norton was 1 in 80 through the tunnel, the track inside was on a curve and the rails were frequently wet. "The water was dripping down all the time." "It was a greasy old tunnel to go through with a heavy load. You couldn't get speed up from a standing start", recalled Horace Slatter. A. ATTEWELL

returned as a passenger train at 9.35 a.m. "I never actually saw the train shunting but I'm pretty sure the wagons off the early-morning goods from Park Royal were fitted and between the engine and the coach." In the 1920s the train consisted of box vans of wool and wagons of roadstone followed by the gaslit brake compo (which officially should have been behind the engine) and at the rear a goods brake van. It was invariably worked by an aged 0–6–0 tender engine. On arrival in the up platform, the engine took water while parcels were unloaded. It appears that after platform work, the train set back from the up platform to the line in front of the goods shed, 'the yard loop', where the wagons were detached and drawn forward into the up platform again, then set back into the shed. The engine then drew forward again and ran round to the other end of the train, collected the brake van, which was put on the shed road, then propelled the coach to the down platform for the return journey empty to Kingham. If required, the engine was used to position wagons in the yard, including those which had arrived off the previous evening's train from Kingham.

The goods brought in on the mixed train consisted mainly of items for the town, which were delivered by cartage agent Johnston. "We used to sort the items into piles around the deck, each representing a shop or business. After several had been done, Charlie handed me the invoices which he had either removed from behind the wagon labels or from a clip board, if they had arrived earlier, and I took these into the goods office and prepared the delivery sheets while Charlie carried on sorting ready for the delivery rounds. We had one sheet per item and numbered the invoice and delivery sheets with the same number as a cross reference. After doing this, I returned to the shed deck and repeated the process until they were all complete, and the delivery sheets were left in the office for collection by the agent who started his rounds at about 9.30 a.m."

Archie later sorted the invoices into alphabetical order by destination and numbered in sequence. "We ended up with an enormous amount of paperwork and bundles were made up with pins through them and old wagon labels in the corners of the pads for reinforcement."

When the shed duties were complete, Archie met the 10.30 a.m. Banbury to

Looking down the Worcester Road towards Moreton-in-Marsh. The bridge over the railway is just apparent in the dip whilst the entrance to the station approach road was on the left, just beyond the parked car. The entrance to the town's cemetery can be seen to the right beyond the bridge. The imposing horse-chestnut trees still make this a beautiful approach to the town today. AUTHOR'S COLLECTION

The northern face of the blue-brick arch bridge carrying the Worcester road over the cutting outside the tunnel. J. H. RUSSELL

The opposite side of the Worcester Road bridge and the short cutting to the tunnel in 1947. Former Banbury engineman Doug Cunningham recalls "When restarting an up goods train after taking water, some men made it the practice to set back and take a run at the tunnel which was very wet and slippery inside". The up starting signal was situated at the end of the down platform for better sighting. The shunt arm on the same post, authorising movements beyond the signal for shunting purposes only, was added sometime after 1926 and was eventually replaced by a calling-on arm.

J. H. RUSSELL

S

Detail views of the 3,000-gallon pillar tank at the north end of the up platform. This was one of a pair provided in 1887. A. ATTEWELL

Kingham auto-car which arrived at 11.20 and helped to unload parcels traffic. "In the summer months, an Eldorado ice-cream man, with a distinctive blue and white boater and tricycle, travelled out on this train from Banbury and we helped him get his bike out of the brake van. Incidentally, the bike had large wheels at the front and a single wheel at the back, over which was a seat – the ice cream was stored in a box at the front. He used to go into the town and I saw him during my lunch break, usually at the top of New Street or near the Burford crossroads – he went back on the 5.20 p.m. Banbury car, after I had gone home, so I didn't see him any more." Kingham clerk Arthur Kilebie's wife used the 11.20 departure to ferry her husband's dinner to Kingham. She packed it in a covered basket and handed it to the guard and Arthur met the train at the end of its journey. "The arrangement went well until Arthur and one of the usual guards fell out. When Mrs. Kilebie arrived the next day, the guard was awkward and decided to charge the dinner as a parcel. It appears this arrangement then came to an end, at least on certain days!"

Archie spent the rest of the morning covering weighbridge duties. On Monday he carried out signal lamping and walked through the tunnel. "I always made sure I had an old lamp with me for light and went in after the 'Ports to Ports Express' – the 'Great Central' as we called it – had cleared around midday."

He went to lunch at 1 o'clock, then "after having my sandwiches and tea in the weighbridge hut, I went up the town and saw my mate Nelson Bubb who worked for the International Stores. We used to walk around the shops and sometimes had half a pint in one of the local pubs."

When he returned at 2 o'clock, Archie went round the yard with Charlie to ensure the wagons were labelled and their flaps secured in readiness for the afternoon goods, which called between 2.50 p.m. and 5.35 p.m. Empty wagons were sometimes marked 'MT' in chalk to the left of the wagon door from the yard side and either taken on to Kingham or returned to Banbury where a lot of the local coal empties were 'pooled' for return to the collieries.

When the afternoon goods arrived in the down platform, the engine took water "which gave me the opportunity to walk along the six foot and remove labels from our wagons." 'Nobby' Clerk was one of the regular Banbury guards on the goods. The train then drew forward clear of the points at the Kingham end and set back in front of the goods shed. "Sometimes she went right back on the stops at the station end." The station truck and the Chipping Norton wagons that were behind the engine were uncoupled from the rest of the train, drawn forward and used to collect outward wagons. The wagons for

Wandering around Chipping Norton station was a wonderful experience, particularly with all the surrounding grass and trees. Photographs rarely do justice to the site but this snapshot from the footpath behind the down platform conveys something of the intimate atmosphere. The Mogul shunting in the background was probably a Kingham–Banbury goods. COLLECTION ALAN BRAIN

This view from the Worcester Road bridge shows both platforms and the goods yard beyond. The train standing on the yard loop with the brake van on the steps of the end loading dock was probably the Kingham goods which was set back there prior to sorting the yard. R. WOODFIN

each siding were left 'on the engine' while outgoing wagons were collected and placed on the shed road as each shunt was made. Wagons of coal for Bliss's and the gas works were taken out onto the running line where they were run round and propelled to the private sidings, the loaded wagons again being used to collect the empties which were assembled on the running lines. When work at the private sidings was complete, the empties were run round and propelled into the yard where they were put onto the cut of outward wagons waiting on the shed road. Any for the Kingham direction were attached to the train whilst those for Banbury were set back through the shed and assembled at the station end for collection on the return journey. The inward wagons were then shunted into position and the engine returned to the train which continued to Kingham. Ample time was allowed for shunting coal wagons to the Gas Works Siding and Bliss's Mill, but

The lattice footbridge, Worcester Road bridge and tunnel viewed from the down platform in 1947. J. H. RUSSELL

A closer view of the footbridge steps and the trees which had been planted along the boundary between the road to Bliss Mill and the grass bank behind the up platform. A. ATTEWELL

The station building was a larger version of those at Adderbury, Bloxham and Hook Norton, though here the forecourt elevation featured a shallower version of the central recessed section common to the platform elevations of them all. Also in each case the gents lavatory end of the others was narrower than the rest of the building, resulting in an offset ridge, whereas the Chipping Norton building was full width at both ends and, interestingly, the canopy valancing was more decorative. The shadows beneath the canopy in this romantic winter view of 1947 make it difficult to discern the detail, but, starting from this end, the pair of windows nearest to the camera illuminated the booking office, whilst in the recess just beyond was a double doorway leading from the booking hall out onto the platform. Next was a window looking out from the general waiting room followed by a door into the ladies waiting room and lavatory. The next window belonged to the ladies waiting room, then the next pair of windows beyond the recess had frosted glass to illuminate the gentlemen's lavatory. Access to the gents was via a door in the end wall where there was also a narrow window with frosted glass, followed by another doorway into the porters room where they also kept lamps and their bicycles. When the GWR introduced their own bus service in 1929, this room had served as an office for the bus staff.
J. H. RUSSELL

CHIPPING NORTON SIGNAL BOX

Of all the signal boxes provided by the Gloucester Wagon Co. in 1887, the one at Chipping Norton was the only one to survive until the end. When there were two boxes, East and West, this one had initially housed a 10-lever frame, but when the West box closed on 13th August 1929, the frame in the East box was replaced with a 3-bar VT 4in 28-lever frame. Fred Warren recalled "The funny thing about Chipping Norton station is that they never had a company telephone in the booking office – they used to come to the box . . . all the telephone messages used to come to the signalman in the box . . . we were forever taking messages down to the office." The public telephone went through to either the goods office or booking office, depending on the position of the switch. Fred Warren recalled when answering the telephone in the goods shed, they would say "Chipping Norton goods station" and if the caller wanted the passenger station, "Hold on and we'll put you through". They would then put the phone down and turn a little lever which rang a bell in the booking office, or vice-versa if the call was to go from the booking office to the goods shed.

S. J. DICKSON

This Nissen-style corrugated-iron shed was used as a military post for soldiers during the Second World War when the railway was very busy handling large stocks of ammunition which was stored in various locations around the town. Fred Warren was a signalman after the war and remembers the hut being used as a staff messroom following the establishment of 'Chippy' as a goods zonal sub-railhead. However, an official document dated June 1947 suggests the shed was used as a parcel office. C. B. SWALLOW

The forecourt elevation of the station building, probably during the early 1950s. The pair of windows on the left served the booking/parcels office. The boarded-up lower right-hand window resulted from a game of football inside the office using a toilet roll as a ball. The damage was blamed on a roll of tweed which was supposed to have inadvertently struck the window. This end of the office was used for the storage of parcels, which were piled all along the wall beneath the window. The centre of the office was occupied by a large desk shared by the clerks and the station master whilst there was a fireplace against the gable end wall. Entry to the station was through the double doorway just out of sight here in the recess. Inside a door on the left gave access to the booking office and further along on the left was a small ticket hatch whilst on the right-hand wall, opposite the booking office door, was the door leading into the general waiting room where there were seats around a table and a fireplace which the porters kept going during the winter. Exit from the booking hall onto the platform was through the double doors mentioned on page 325.
LENS OF SUTTON

Another view of the station in 1947, this time from the footbridge. Female goods clerk Frances Flick (née Kitching) recalls that Fred Oates kept the garden from 1948 and that there was apparently an ornamental lavatory pan (ex-LNER) "next to the shelter" planted with flowers. J. H. RUSSELL

Archie recalls "They were certainly not shunted every day – more likely once a week."

The time taken for the shunting varied according to the traffic but the running line had to be clear for the passage of the 9.30 a.m. Newcastle to Swansea express which passed through Chipping Norton at 4.9 p.m., only calling when required. This was usually arranged in advance when tickets were issued, the train being checked at the home signal and the driver sounding his whistle to acknowledge that he was required to stop. A piano tuner from Cheltenham often arrived at the station on the offchance of catching the train. Otherwise he travelled on the 4.3 p.m. from Banbury, changing at Kingham.

"Later in the afternoon I removed one set of labels from the newly arrived wagons of coal and in addition to recording details in my wagon book, which I kept in the weighbridge office, I sent each merchant advice notes to confirm how long they had available before we raised demurrage charges. The top copy of these notes were blue and the bottom one pink. They were laid out in columns, the one on the left for the date of arrival and the next when the truck was empty. There was a printed note on the top of the advice as a reminder of the demurrage arrangements whereby the wagon had to be emptied within three days. As soon as practicable, I got the merchant to sign my book to confirm receipt of the wagon/s – it might be possible to give them an advice note at the same time, otherwise I simply put the notes through the coal office letter boxes in the yard. The only one I posted was in connection with the

Early pictures show that the up platform, seen on the left, had been fenced all along its rear edge. However, some time after the First World War, probably in the early 1920s, the fence was removed to provide an area for a station garden, presumably prompted by the spirit of competition between the other stations along the line. The impressive results are seen in Vol. 1, but with economies in staff and then the Second World War, the gardens fell into decline. This 1947 view shows the tidy scene, but the spirit had gone. J. H. RUSSELL

A 1950s close-up of the station nameboard and platform seat. J. H. MOSS

Those who knew the station before it was demolished will find few pictures which can do justice to the intimate beauty of the setting. This c.1947 view manages to convey something of the atmosphere of the site. The corrugated-iron hut behind the platform fence near the signal box was a lamp room. The hut had a door on the signal box side with a large oil drum inside and a shelf. The oil drum was tapped and lasted a considerable time as it was only used for the weekly signal lamp change. The drum arrived on the station truck and took two men to lift it into position off the floor on to wooden blocks. The 3,000-gallon pillar tank, 9ft diameter, 8ft deep with 6in swing jib, at this end of the down platform was the other one of the pair provided in 1887.

R. WOODFIN

No. 6167 at Chipping Norton in 1947 with what must have been the 3.10 Chipping Norton to Oxford train. The engine and coaches were probably substituting for the diesel railcar which was scheduled for this service. J. H. RUSSELL

occasional load for Pratt and Haynes. When the wagon/s had been emptied, I got the merchant's rep to sign and date my book. They had monthly checks of the book from our office to see if any demurrage charges were due." Incidentally, Archie also maintained another record book for general traffic which was kept in the goods office. "The wagon books – about 9 inches by 12 inches – were laid out in columns with the date the wagon arrived on the left, where it had come from, the consignee, wagon number, and on the right a space for the date and signature when it had been emptied. Charlie used the books to prepare the rolling stock returns and they were also scrutinised by Fred Darke."

In the meantime, loads were being brought in from the town, some of which were forwarded on the goods train which was due to leave at 5.35 p.m. after the arrival of the 5.20 autocar from Kingham.

Archie finished his shift in the parcels office where he prepared consignments for despatch. "Bill Johnson, one of Johnstons' delivery men, always came back at around 4 o'clock with loads of tweed from Bliss's and, using a chart in the office, I calculated the charges and stuck parcel stamps on each consignment. Madge Tustian would help me if she was in the office but if helping out in the goods, as was often the case, Mr. Williams came in and gave me a hand. I loaded the packages on to the 4.56 p.m. train to Kingham, which I caught home."

PARCELS

The most regular inwards traffic was of a perishable nature, including crates of fish from Grimsby, which were transhipped to the 6.22 a.m. auto-car at Banbury.

Outwards traffic included regular consignments of tweed in 65 yard lengths from Bliss's Mill. This was very cumbersome to handle. Archie Warren remembers "nearer the war, a lot of army khaki and RAF blue material was sent away." Other parcels traffic received included items from Great Universal Stores and Littlewoods whilst pheasant eggs from William George Bayliss, a poultry breeder in the Banbury Road, were sent to large houses and the birds bred for 'the shoot' – "we used to send the eggs during late spring/early summer."

The late-turn porter, Charlie Parsons, worked on a 1.45 to 9.45 p.m. shift so he dealt with the return pick-up goods. When the goods train returned from Kingham, it was booked to call at Chipping Norton between 7.18 and 7.42 p.m. On arrival, it stopped short of the yard exit points at the station end where the train was secured on the running line and the engine and station truck were detached and set back into the shed road to collect the cut of wagons left there earlier and attach them to the front of the train. Any inwards wagons from Kingham were left on the shed road for positioning the next day.

In the 1920s, the up goods was run directly into the yard loop where the train was secured. The engine drew forward and set back into the shed road to collect the outwards wagons for return to Banbury. The 'outwards cut' had usually been left ready for collection at the Banbury end of the 'shed wagons' which were drawn into position before being uncoupled and left in position inside the

The station from the goods shed, showing the loading dock at the end of the yard loop. The dock was primarily used for loading bales of hay from lorries backed up to open wagons. In Fred Warren's time, timber was stacked alongside the shed road, on the right, by Messrs. Claridges who had a depot at Heythrop. Locally-felled supplies were taken to the station in horse-drawn carts and subsequently loaded onto a Macaw by two railway loaders from Worcester, using a rail-mounted crane. The wooden enclosure on the right was used for the storage of station coal which, in traditional manner, was unloaded by permanent way staff each year from a wagon left alongside. The pathway climbing away from behind the up platform to connect with Mill Road, was used by women workers at Bliss's Mill, who travelled in from Bloxham and Sarsden. The staff token apparatus alongside both up and down lines feature in this view. Fred says it was only used now and then when the Swansea and Newcastle trains were not required to call, otherwise exchanges were carried out with the signalman on the platform.
J. H. RUSSELL

Looking east over the site of the original terminus which became a conventional goods yard. From left to right this c.1950 view features the very top of the pillar tank at the down platform, the up inner home signal, the small weighbridge office, the stables, 4-stall cattle pens and goods shed. The earthworks in the foreground indicate the original alignment of the Worcester Road, altered c.1600. J. H. RUSSELL

This c.1950 view with No. 5361 on the goods loop provides a glimpse of the coal yard and Atkinson's and Welford's coal offices. J. H. RUSSELL

building ready for unloading the next day. The outwards wagons were then drawn out into the up platform and set back onto the remainder of the train waiting in the loop. When these moves were completed, the engine pulled the train into the up platform where it took water before continuing on its journey to Banbury. The last autocar from Banbury arrived at 8.30 p.m., then reappeared on the return journey, leaving Kingham at 8.55 p.m. After it had gone, Charlie locked up the station, turned off the lights and, on the way back to his home in The Leys, stopped to turn off the lights on the foot crossing.

Geoff Rose joined the Chipping Norton staff as a goods clerk in 1940. He was sixteen years old, his one previous job having been an assistant at Hartwells ironmongers in the High Street.

At that time the staff comprised:

Station master – William Williams
Ticket and parcels clerk – Violet (Madge) Tustian
Porters – Charlie Hall (foreman and goods checker); George Smith; Charlie Parsons
Goods Dept. – Fred Darke (chief goods clerk) and Geoff Rose (goods clerk)
Signalmen – Fred Jones and Ben Collins

Working from 8.0 a.m. till 5.0 p.m. with an hour for lunch, Geoff and his supervisor Fred Darke were responsible for the receipt and despatch of goods. He recalls that the mornings were largely occupied in handling goods received from the previous evening's train. Porter George Smith was responsible for unloading the wagons in the shed whilst Charlie Hall, the checker, would tally the goods with the consignment note attached to the wagon. He then took the invoice into Geoff, who recorded it in the inwards counter book and entered it on a delivery note. If the items were collected from the station, the recipient simply signed the inwards counter book at the shed. However, Geoff recalls that during the war years, most of the goods were delivered by Johnston cartage agents whose driver Bill Johnson used a single horse-drawn four-wheel vehicle for smaller parcels, or Len Morris, who used a two-horse dray for heavier goods.

When the cartage agents returned from their rounds, consignment notes were prepared for the goods they had brought in for despatch. The porters were responsible for loading whilst Charlie Hall would

GOODS TRAFFIC

Cement

Occasionally a box van containing bags of Portland cement arrived and was unloaded near the cattle pens. It was stored in a grounded railway van body, and collected by local builders merchants as required.

Roadstone/chippings

Ardsheal Quarry, Argyll, Sent regular wagonloads of roadstone to Chipping Norton for council road improvement schemes. Most of the work was undertaken in the summer months, the stone being delivered to the various sites by a Mr. Watton using a Foden lorry.

Tar

Again in connection with road work, tar arrived in a tank wagon, the contents being discharged into metal tubs using an iron tube fixed to the discharge point under the tank. When necessary to ensure the free-running of the contents, a makeshift brazier, using a bucket punched with holes, was placed under the pipe. Watton also delivered the barrels to the various sites of work, a Mr. Williams being responsible for discharging the contents. As a precaution, the tank was discharged near the cattle pens in case water might be needed quickly to quench any fire.

Archie Warren recalls a Mr. Melton receiving gravel and tar in connection with local road resurfacing schemes. The tar was in barrels and was apparently ready to spray on the road with the gravel following behind. "This used to be dealt with right over the back of the yard on the road behind the old engine shed which, incidentally, was still there but overgrown."

Bones/fat

Regular lorry loads of loose animal bones were weighed and despatched to Gloucester for the manufacture of glue. The bones came from the Heythrop Hounds, Worcester Road, after the meat had been boiled off and fed to the dogs. Fred Warren kept the weighbridge hut door shut because of the smell! Barrels of fat resulting from the above were occasionally sent out in the station truck by a Mr. Lines.

In the late 1930s bones were despatched to the Sheppey Glue and Chemical Works, Queenborough on the Isle of Sheppey in Kent.

Metal castings

The Hub Ironworks Co. Ltd. in the High Street produced various items including manhole covers and pulleys for railway signal wires. Most of these items were sent loose in the station truck. Very occasionally a wagon of pig iron arrived for the works.

Hay

Hay was despatched by local agent, Mr. Newton of Hook Norton. Bales were handled at the end loading dock with Newton supervising the loading. Most of this traffic was, however, dealt with at Hook Norton.

COAL MERCHANTS

Coal and coke supplies came principally from Baddesley, Markham Main and Nuneaton pits with lesser quantities from Wales. Chipping Norton Co-operative Society was the largest user.

Chipping Norton Co-operative Society

Established in the mid-1880s, the Co-operative Society's first shop was in the High Street. It became the Chipping Norton Co-operative Society around the time of the Great War and in the early 1920s expanded, with additional premises

The 6-stall stable which faced the end of the goods sidings was authorised in August 1904 'to accommodate the Co's horses in the goods yard'. The recommended establishment for cartage was '4 horses @ £55 each, 4 sets of harnesses at £6 each, 1 lorry @ £50, 1 float @ £50, 1 parcels van @ £56. Employment of 3 carriers, erection of 6-stall stable £433. Annual cost to company will be £438 10s 3d.' When the cartage and delivery work was taken over by W. Johnston around 1921, the 40ft x 21ft building became redundant and was eventually converted into a garage for the GWR buses which commenced in July 1929, primarily by the provision of a double-door opening in the west-facing gable end. This was later used by the Zonal delivery lorries.
COLLECTION B. HOPER

The brick weighbridge office dated back to the original terminus. In 1927 a circular noted the change from a 10-ton cart weighbridge (No. 2855) 10ft x 6ft to a 20-ton cart weighbridge (No. 7242) 10ft x 8ft. The dimension was probably a misprint as a 1938 document lists the same machine number as measuring 18ft x 8ft. Fred Warren recalled, "We had a weighbridge boy and on occasions when he wasn't there, the lorry drivers used to stand there sounding the horn and we had to whip up there from the goods shed." If it was pouring with rain, there would be an argument over who had to go — "It was the only time we'd fight." The lad porter used the place as his office. It was equipped with a table and chair and records were maintained here of wagons dealt with.
A. ATTEWELL

opening at Market Place and West Street. A coal office and bays were located at the station. Archie Warren recalls "they had their own wagons and three lorries. They usually had three or four wagons in at once and often could not clear them in time so dumped the coal on the ground to avoid demurrage." At one time their supplies are said to have come from Haunchwood.

Walker and Atkinson

This concern was shown in 1906 local directories as coal, corn and seed merchants in the High Street, a John Walker running the business since it had been established around the turn of the century. Atkinson appears to have taken over in the mid-1920s when, according to local directories, he only dealt in corn. However, Fred Warren remembers the firm trading in coal under their full name in 1929. They are said to have been a Shipston-on-Stour firm, who held wharfage at the station as well as an office in Cattle Market.

Jeffries

J. W. Jeffries of 17 High Street, had become a coal merchant by 1927, local directories listing his address as the High Street with a depot at the railway station. He was earlier described as a saddler and harness maker. Jeffries' coal is said to have come from Baddesley. He also dealt in coke and is recalled as supplying 100 tons to Cornwell Manor, and 50 tons for Dean, near Charlbury. The coke came from Banbury. Brasseys of Heythrop had a 10-ton truck every month.

Frost

This Banbury company had no shop in the town, just an order office alongside their wharfage in the goods yard.

Archie also recalls that Johnston, the cartage agent, received coal and that "we also had an occasional load for Pratt and Haynes of Shipton-under-Wychwood. This was all for one customer so didn't have to go over the bridge." Archie remembers all the merchants, except Pratt & Haynes, had offices in the yard, the Co-op having a concrete stacking ground near the old railway stables. Coke was received occasionally although most was supplied by the local gas works.

These two photographs show Co-op staff in the goods yard, probably during the 1920s. The top photograph features the side of the engine shed which was still open at this time. The men in the lower photo were (from left to right) back row: Mr. Latham, Jesse Hadland and Tom Hill. Front row: Alf Doman, foreman Charlie Winnet and Jack Bolter. Charlie Winnet also appears in the top photograph immediately in front of the horse. CTY. ALAN BRAIN

GREAT WESTERN RAILWAY.

ADVICE OF COAL, COKE AND PATENT FUEL TRAFFIC.

Mr.
Messrs. Jeffries

C. Norton STATION, 22/3/43

The undermentioned wagons having arrived at this station consigned to you, I have to request that you will please for them to be unloaded at once, and I give you notice that unless they are released on or before 6.0 a.m. on 24/3 (whether the wagons are standing on the sidings available for unloading or in other sidings by reason of your being un take delivery), Demurrage will be charged you from that time at the rate of 3/0d. per wagon per day.

For the GREAT WESTERN RAILWAY COMPANY,

J.W.S.

FROM	TRUCK NUMBERS	DESCRIPTION OF TRAF
Bedworth.		
Arley	11512.	
	2350	Coal

PHONE—CHIPPING NORTON 67

TELEGRAMS—JEFFRIES, CHIPPING N

BOT. OF

J. W. JEFFRIES & SONS

(J. W. JEFFRIES, PROPRIETOR)

81

ORDERS RECEIVED AT 17 HIGH STREET

COAL & COKE MERCHANTS

No. 17 HIGH STREET
CHIPPING NORTON

WHARF: STATION, G.W.R.

May 31 1929

15/- £ 1 14 .

Produced at AUDIT HUBERT LEICESTER & Co. Chartered Accountants

J. W. JEFFRIES,
CHIPPING NORTON

3244. July 16

Received *with thanks from*
Mrs Hitchman

1 : 14 :

J. W. JEFFRIES

Jeffries' lorry and staff.

E. F. W. JOHNSTON

G.W.R. Agent, General Haulier and Furniture Remover

47 West Street, CHIPPING NORTON

Coventry-born Ernest Frederick William Johnston, known as William, moved with his family to Chipping Norton around 1900. He had been brought up at Stratford upon Avon where he became a saddler. By 1907 he was trading at 6 West Street where he also made boots and shoes to order. William's sons Reg and Edgar helped their father, but the haulage side of the business, which had certainly begun by about 1920, was in the hands of his eldest son, Ernest William David, known as David.

Apart from general haulage work, Johnstons succeeded in obtaining the railway cartage agency, probably around 1920/21. They took over the work from the GWR, which represented a very unusual arrangement as the reverse was the norm. They retained the agency until the introduction of the GWR Zonal Delivery Scheme in 1948.

Meanwhile, in 1917 William had inherited several hundred pounds, part of which was evidently used to purchase a property at 45/47 West Street, where stables and later garages were built. The horses had previously been kept in Burford Road.

When William died in 1933, the business passed to his three sons. In 1948 the haulage business was absorbed by British Road Services and not long afterwards, in 1951, the coal business became a company trading as E. F. W. Johnston Ltd.

When Ernest died in 1951 the business continued under Reg and Edgar who, after selling out to Welfords in 1960, continued to manage the business until 1968.

E. F. W. Johnston.

A carnival photo, probably taken in the 1920s, showing one of Johnston's carts being used as a float to advertise the GWR. This picture also shows Johnston's shop at 6 West Street in the background, E. F. W. Johnston standing in the centre and his son David holding the reins behind.

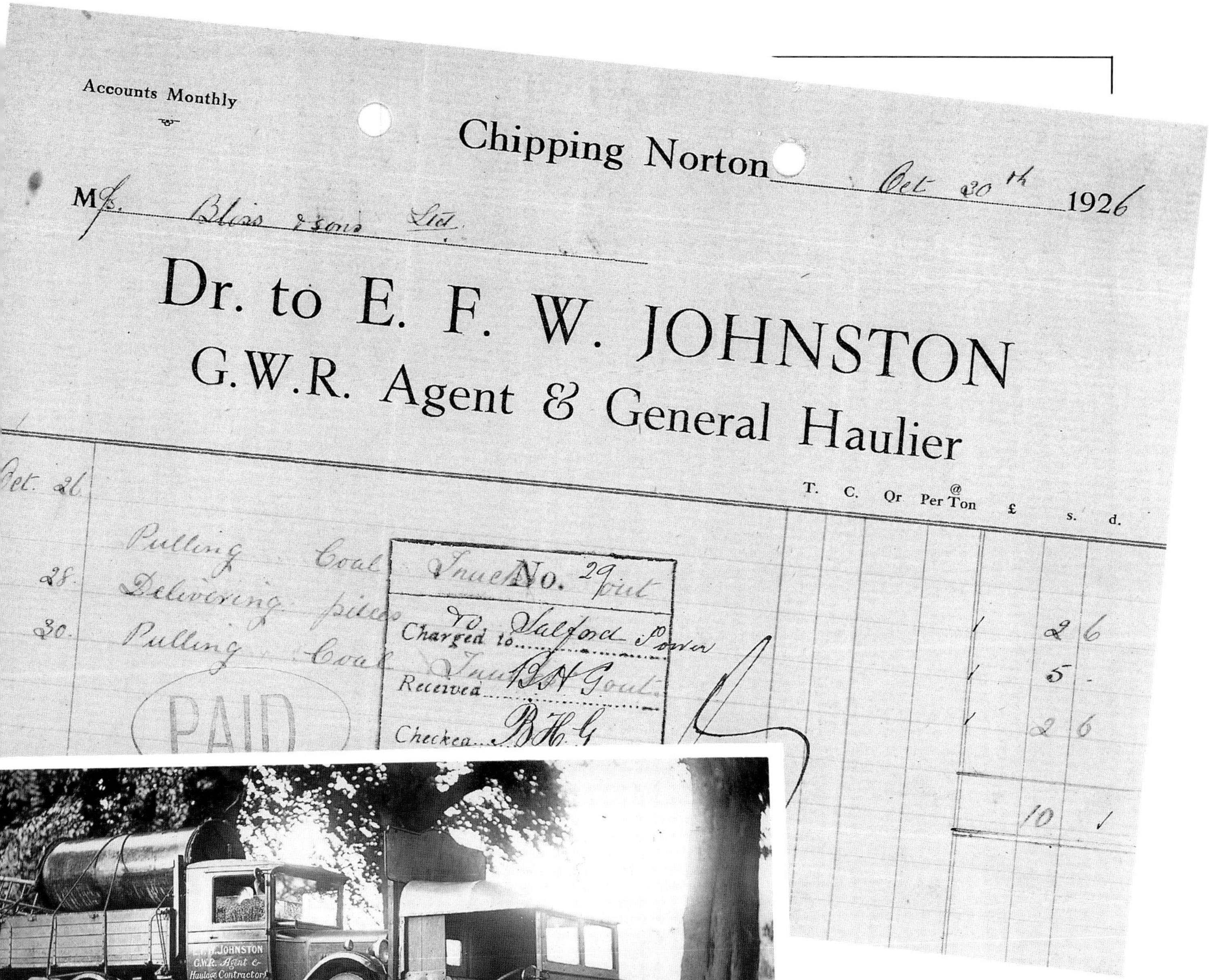
Accounts Monthly

Chipping Norton ......Oct 30th...... 1926

M/s. ......Bliss & Sons Ltd......

Dr. to E. F. W. JOHNSTON
G.W.R. Agent & General Haulier

		T.	C.	Qr	Per @ Ton	£	s.	d.
Oct. 26	Pulling Coal Truck No. 29 out					1	2	6
28.	Delivering pieces To Charged to Salford Power					1	5	-
30.	Pulling Coal Truck Received BH Gout. Checked BHG					1	2	6
							10	1

PAID

Two of Johnston's lorries in 1930, one loaded on the other for a carnival procession. The left-hand figure leaning against the lorry was Bill Johnson, the central one is unrecorded whilst the one on the right was Ernest Johnston.

A glimpse of the cab of one of Johnston's lorries showing the style of lettering.

ALL PHOTOS CTY. BERYL JOHNSTON

Detail views of the weigh-bridge office. The adjacent petrol pump was transferred from Shipton under Wychwood in 1948 for fuelling the Zonal delivery lorries. A. ATTEWELL

The south-west and south-east elevations. A. ATTEWELL

The red-brick goods shed was built by the Great Western c.1887 to replace the one at the original terminus. It was a variation of a standard design used at Maidenhead, Twyford and Tetbury. According to an official survey after closure, the building measured 102ft x 36ft whilst the office was 21ft x 17ft. Frances Flick recalls "It was quite a big office and we had sloping desks all round with a lip at the bottom to stop your pens falling off . . . and high stools." With windows on three sides, "you could see right up the track" and on the wall against the main building there was a hatch "through which paperwork was passed" and a door. Of the late 1930s Archie Warren recalls a central table in the office and that the attic room above was reached with a ladder and used to store old records. Public access was via the steps seen on the left, then a door on the right led off the landing into the office where there was a counter and flap, a section of which was removed and refixed in a new position at right-angles and in line with the door frame.

R. A. STARES

fix a label to the wagon identifying its destination.

All invoices were sent out at the end of the month by Fred Darke, including those for coal wharfage, but any cash transactions were dealt with at the station booking office.

After Geoff had been there for ten or eleven months, Madge Tustian left and he replaced her as booking clerk at the station, working from 7.0 a.m. to 5.45 p.m. He recalls that between the departure of the first down autocar at 7.15 a.m. and its return, he took a 45minute break for breakfast.

Traffic figures for the war years show a substantial increase in tickets sold with weekly averages of 218 to 580. Parcels fell slightly with 247 to 318 received each week and 61 to 114 despatched, whilst coal remained at pre-war levels with an average of 374 tons per week for 1939 and 1941–2. General merchandise received was not very different to pre-war levels with averages of between 98 and 120 tons per week but the forwarded tonnage rose to between 32 and 146 tons a week, with, in 1944 only, an exceptional average of 337 tons per week. 'Other minerals' forwarded averaged between 10 and 20 tons per week and those received ranged from 41 to 94 tons per week.

The arrival of the 50th Division Territorials, the Durham Light Infantry, in the area in 1940 brought about large numbers of soldiers arriving at and departing from Chipping Norton station, often creating long queues at the booking office. When they were going home to County Durham on leave, the army gave the GWR 24 hours notice, a despatch rider arriving at the station with a list of up to thirty names of personnel and the destinations required. Geoff had the task of selecting the cheapest and most efficient route, which was time-consuming, especially if an emergency line closure meant a hurried search for an alternative route. Making out tickets for all of the names on the list could well involve an hour or more's work. When completed, the base was notified and the despatch rider would collect the tickets. No cash was exchanged as the tickets were charged to the War Department; the following day the personnel were dropped off at the station in a lorry.

On a cold and snowy Sunday at the end of 1940, the division was despatched on active service, William Williams noting that there was no rejoicing.

From around 1942 a number of women were employed at Chipping Norton station. Joan Keeley, Nancy Heath and Beryl Shepherd all worked in the goods office under the supervision of George Smith. Nancy Hiatt was a checker but the girls also carried out general porters duties as required.

In 1943, 14-year old Pete Scarsbrook began at Chipping Norton as a weighbridge boy/lad porter, whilst Monty Harding became a GWR lorry driver, Frank White helped out in the booking office and John Smart was appointed as a lad porter.

One of Pete's memories is helping Monty, to load the lorry with regular consignments of flour in crates for Bignells, the corner cafe in New Street. He also recalls the arrival of the Royal Army Ordnance Corps who unloaded ammunition which arrived by rail and that when the Americans first arrived, they used the weighbridge office until a Nissen hut was built for them alongside the station build-

The interior of the goods shed, looking towards Kingham. By the time of this photograph, several alterations had taken place in connection with the Zonal Collection and Delivery Scheme, under which Chipping Norton became one of the sub-railheads of Oxford. These included 'Excavating and concreting in foundations for crane; concrete foundations to widened cart berth; additional brickwork; new steel lintels and stanchions; buffer beams to cart berths and bay; additional verandah covering; make good timber decking; break up existing concrete foundations, take out brickwork and make good; alterations to guttering, pipes and drainage connections; dismantling displaced works; replacement cost of 5 iron framed windows displace and not reproduced; remove 6-ton fixed hand crane FM4264 from Shipton and re-erect at Chipping Norton'. The two 30 cwt cranes Nos. FM843 and 844 were officially listed as pre-1914 but whether they were the originals is not known. The wooden panelling in the left-hand corner enclosed an office which doubled as a mess room for the porters and a store for the goods checker's paperwork. There was a desk, a long bench and chairs inside.

R. A. STARES

The forecourt elevation of the goods shed, showing the loading bays after the 1948 alterations for the Zonal Delivery Scheme which included the additional verandah covering.
COLLECTION B. P. HOPER

The 30 cwt dormant weighing machine in the foreground, No. 4446, was moved from Exeter where it had become redundant. It was a modern version of an earlier appliance, 32 cwt dormant weighing machine No. 2856. The goods office was reached via the door in the end wall. The office was connected to the shed deck by means of a small hatchway which Fred remembers as 'not used a lot' in 1929. However, in this picture the hatch is obscured by an internal timber-built office which is also believed to have been provided in connection with the Zonal Scheme. The door in the wall above the crane led to the loft of the shed office and, as described in the text, was reached by a ladder. Prior to the Zonal alterations, each of the rail and road openings were closed by sliding doors. The shed interior was illuminated by two paraffin vapour Tilley floodlights which were installed in 1948, also in connection with the Zonal Scheme, whilst the gas lighting in the goods office was altered and improved at the same time. Whether or not there was some problem with the Tilley lamps is not known but by September 1949 electric lighting had been installed.
R. A. STARES

The south-facing gable end and forecourt elevations of the much altered red-brick goods shed in 1950. The brackets on the end wall were provided for firebuckets, as seen on page 349. The steps in the rail entrance provided access between the shed deck and the yard. There was an equivalent set at the opposite end. J. H. RUSSELL

This view from the lane outside the railway boundary shows the relationship between the goods yard and the Bliss Tweed Mill.
BERYL JOHNSTON

The 6-ton fixed hand crane No. FM4264 was transferred from Shipton in 1948 in connection with the Zonal Scheme. A redundant assets sheet records it as dating from 1939 when presumably it was built and installed at Shipton. Prior to this there was only the usual 1 ton 10cwt crane in the goods shed.
S. J. DICKSON

The water tank on the south-east boundary of the goods yard lingered as a reminder of the former existence of the engine shed which had stood nearby. The wrought-iron tank, measuring 24ft x 12ft x 6ft 6in and supported on cast-iron pillars, was a standard Swindon design provided in 1888. It held 10,800 gallons and, like the two 3,000-gallon pillar tanks, was fed by gravity from a stream in the hills via a reservoir about 400 yds from the station. On more than one occasion when the supply was reduced to a trickle, Charlie Parsons discovered that a dead sheep had blocked the inlet in the field. A. E. SMITH

THE LEYS CHIPPING NORTON

The tree-lined Leys with its Victorian houses features in many pictures of the railway taken from the Common. When station master W. Williams retired on 31st October 1945, the GWR agreed to allow him to remain living at No. 52 as the house was 'not required by his successor'. 'Mr. Williams will pay his rent in at Chipping Norton Station.' Other members of staff also lived in The Leys. This picture was probably taken around 1950.

COLLECTION ALAN BRAIN

This view, looking in the opposite direction towards Banbury in 1947, shows, from left to right, the up and down lines of the crossing loop, the yard loop, shed road, the two yard roads, coal siding and the former engine shed siding. In 1929 the yard road behind the goods shed was used for general traffic such as cement and roadstone as well as serving the cattle pens. The other yard road was used for general traffic and coal. The former engine shed siding was rarely used as there was no road access for loading.

J. H. RUSSELL

This winter view c.1950 shows the fencing and gates protecting the foot-crossing over the railway from The Leys to the Common and Bliss Mill. The road in the foreground gave access from the Worcester Road to the mill. J. H. RUSSELL

No. 5361 shunting the yard in the 1950s. COLLECTION GREAT WESTERN TRUST

ing. Ammunition was stored in the hut and, after the crates in which it arrived were broken up, the wood was stored in the station yard.

Monty Harding asked one of the Americans if he could have some of the wood, and, with permission, he and Pete helped themselves. However, when the other station staff joined in, they were told that it was not permitted and after an inquiry "they took all this wood up to the council yard at Banbury Road and the blokes up there had it, but they never caught me and Monty."

Pete Scarsbrook left Chipping Norton in 1944 and, after a short posting at Kingham station, he joined the army. When station master William Williams retired in 1945, chief goods clerk Fred Darke took over the position.

After the war, the bustle and activity faded away and passenger numbers gradually fell to pre-war levels whereas general merchandise increased. In an attempt to secure more efficiency in the face of ever-increasing road competition, the GWR reorganised deliveries of goods under the Zonal Collection and Delivery Scheme of 1947, under which Chipping Norton became one of the distribution centres. This is detailed in Volume 3. After all the upheaval, Charlie Parsons, who had served the goods department since 1906, retired in 1947, which was also the last year of the Great Western Railway.

Looking towards Kingham in 1947, with the foot crossing running across the centre of the picture, which also features Bliss's main building on the right and the weaving sheds visible behind the siding gate. The siding trailing from the double discs on the up line apparently once served as a loading platform. As can be seen, the footpath crossing was lit by gas lamps on each side of the line. Both the porters Charlie Parsons and George Smith lived at the bottom of The Leys and on dark winter mornings their first job was to light the lamps on their way to the station, extinguishing them at night on their way home after the late shift. J. H. RUSSELL

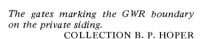

The gates marking the GWR boundary on the private siding.
COLLECTION B. P. HOPER

This view of the west (Kingham) end of the goods yard in the early postwar years represents the scene very much as Fred Warren would have known it. The yard shunting spur is seen at the bottom right whilst the yard itself consisted of a loop between the goods shed and the down line, then the shed road which also formed a loop, followed by the yard roads. The siding behind the shed served the cattle pen but in 1929 was used for general yard traffic such as cement (for the Portland Cement store) and roadstone. The siding alongside was used for general traffic and coal but the next, on which a rake of wagons is seen, tended to be for coal traffic only. The siding at the back of the yard, which had been used in connection with the former engine shed, was rarely used; any wagons not able to be accommodated in the yard were placed out of position in Bliss's siding.

J. H. RUSSELL

This final view of Chipping Norton shows the convergence of the down and up loops on the curve which took the new B&CD away from the old terminus on the new alignment towards Banbury. Once past the up home signal, trains were on the trackbed of the original branch. The permanent way huts can be seen near the base of the signal. J. H. RUSSELL

THE LATER YEARS OF THE BLISS MILL

William Bliss, Chipping Norton's largest employer, had created a working environment where his workers were encouraged to feel that they were members of a large family concern. William Bliss was the most influential figure in the history of the town; instrumental in bringing the railway to the town, he first established the proposal for a Banbury and Cheltenham Railway at the opening of the Chipping Norton Branch in 1856.

Bliss also gave £1,500 towards the rebuilding of the Baptist Chapel, he sponsored the building of the British Schools in New Street and set up a reading room for his staff. As a testimony of his character, Bliss was elected Mayor of Chipping Norton four times, spanning a 28-year period between 1848 and 1869.

Following the death of Bliss in 1883, the mill experienced a chequered history. His son, also William, struggled to keep financial control of the business, having entered into partnership with his brother-in-law, S. F. Flint, which proved unsuccessful. Increasing control by the Birmingham Banking Company led to the entire labour force being paid off during one weekend in 1893; the following Monday, only 300 were re-employed. Following the difficulties in operating the business as a limited company, the family decided to end their 140-year association with the cloth manufactory and left Chipping Norton.

Fortunes turned around to a degree when James Hawkyard, a Bliss employee, and A. H. Dunstan, a Birmingham chartered accountant, became chief directors of the firm. However, employer/employee relations suffered as a result of a bitter 8-month strike during the winter of 1913–14. This was a sad contrast to the diligent concern of William Bliss.

The business was bought from the bank by Dunstan in 1917 and sold in 1920 to Fox Brothers of Wellington, in Somerset. It closed in 1980.

An aerial view of Bliss Mill. COLLECTION ALAN BRAIN

SARSDEN HALT

86m 47c

SARSDEN Halt was a rural outpost situated beside the disused Churchill Mill where the narrow Mill Lane crossed the railway, which at that point was running parallel to the Swailsford or Cornwell Brook. As we have seen in Volume One, a siding was first established here on the original branch line between Chipping Norton Junction and Chipping Norton. However, these notes are concerned with the running of the siding after the halt was opened here in 1906.

Frustratingly, the traffic statistics for Sarsden were included with the figures for Chipping Norton, so once again we are unable to establish the numbers of passengers using the halt or the amount of traffic passing in and out of the siding.

In the 1920s the halt was looked after by William Henry Piper who, in the census for 1891, is recorded as a railway porter aged 22, unmarried and lodging at Churchill. Whether or not he was employed at Sarsden siding at this time is not known. After getting married, he lived with his parents-in-law in Hastings Hill and had four children, but then his wife died. Later he married Georgina Jarvis, a district nurse from Suffolk. They rented accommodation near Ropers Farm, West End, Kingham and raised a daughter called Marjorie, who has kindly helped with the preparation of these notes.

A day at Sarsden Halt in the late 1920s would have begun quietly enough, as William Piper set out from his home in Kingham, and walked the 1½ miles to the halt, first along the Churchill Road, then along the old Swailsford Bridge carriageway, turning onto the Miller's Path, which was part of the road which 'Squire' Young had built to link Kingham Hill with Churchill.

Besides his lunch, he carried bread and milk for the cat, which lived in the brick shed near the Sarsden signal box steps. Marjorie recalls "it was forever having kittens, but none of them ever got run over. We kept a lovely black one."

The signal box, 150ft long sleeper-built platform and corrugated-iron pagoda-style waiting shelter seen against a backdrop of pollarded willows. This photo was taken in 1947 from the entrance to the little goods yard. J. H. RUSSELL

The early shift began at six o'clock, William unlocking the signal box and the weighbridge office. He swept and cleaned the weighbridge as inspections were frequently made and Marjorie recalled "When the inspector came round, if there was any wet on it, he used to grumble."

The early-morning milk delivery brought frantic activity; "All the farmers used to go rushing down here. If one of them was cutting it a bit fine getting to the halt in time, there was scarcely any time left to open the crossing gates before the train arrived."

Regular milk suppliers were Paulins off the Chipping Norton Road, who arrived with a single horse-drawn trap, Kellands of Grange Farm, opposite the war memorial, and Crudges. Milk was taken on the 7.48 a.m. Kingham–Banbury passenger train, which was due to leave Sarsden at 7.54 a.m. Milk was sent six days a week and on Sunday it was taken to Kingham station.

Lamping was a typical duty which was carried out at least weekly. A small shed near the road contained the paraffin for refuelling the lamps. Marjorie recalled her father walking to the distant signal towards the Cornwell Bridge to refuel the lamp there.

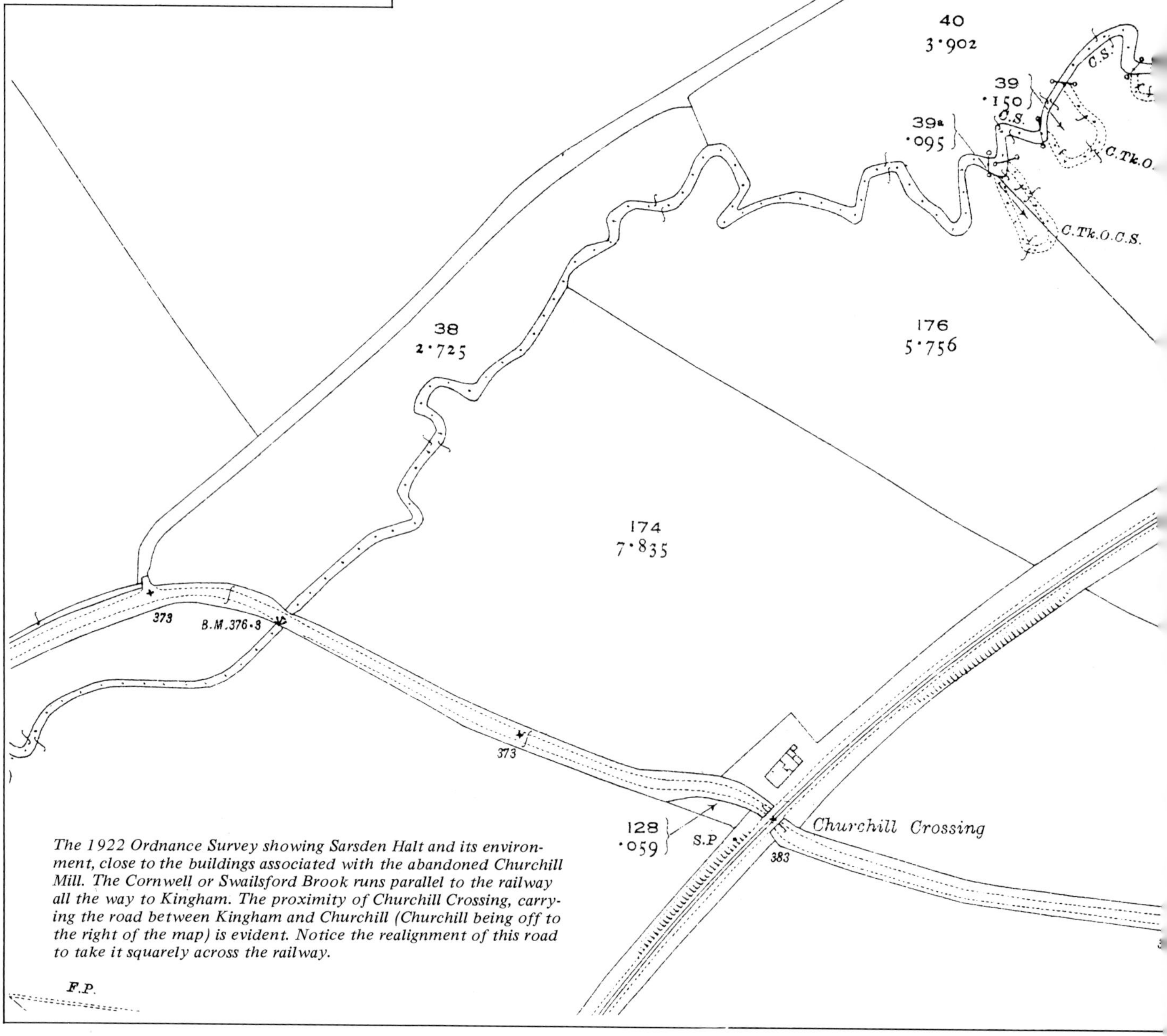

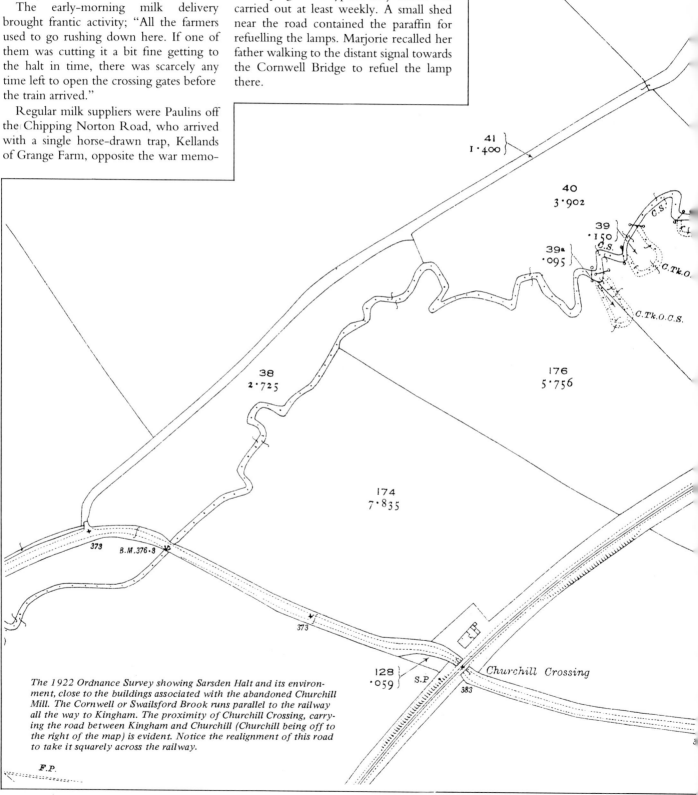

The 1922 Ordnance Survey showing Sarsden Halt and its environment, close to the buildings associated with the abandoned Churchill Mill. The Cornwell or Swailsford Brook runs parallel to the railway all the way to Kingham. The proximity of Churchill Crossing, carrying the road between Kingham and Churchill (Churchill being off to the right of the map) is evident. Notice the realignment of this road to take it squarely across the railway.

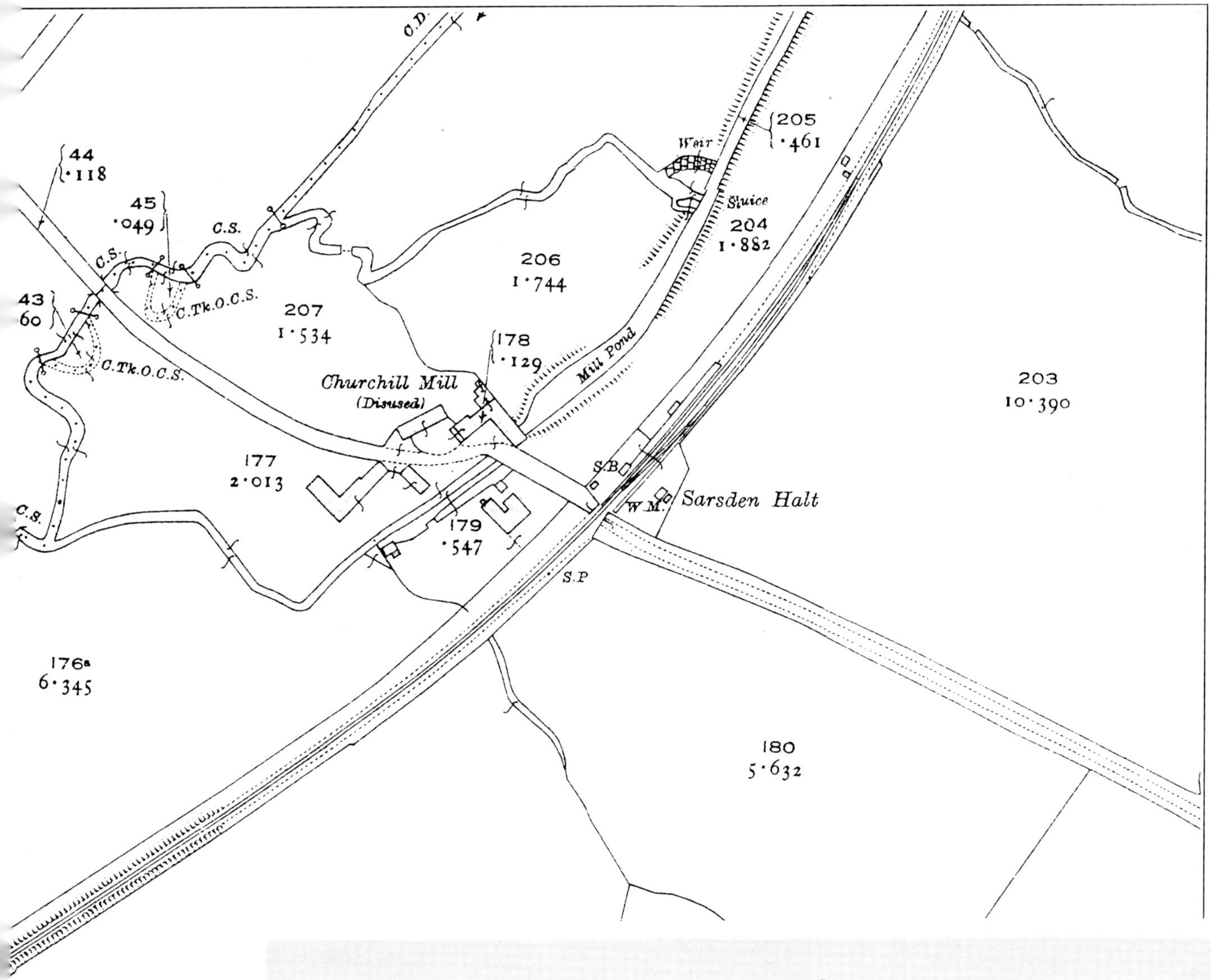

Looking north-east from alongside the goods siding, probably c.1950 with the line towards Chipping Norton curving northwards through the winter landscape. The two-lever ground frame controlling access to this end of the siding is just apparent near the permanent way hut.
J. H. RUSSELL

Looking towards Chipping Norton from the 7ft wide platform of the halt one sunny evening in the late spring of 1947. J. H. RUSSELL

A companion view, looking in the opposite direction towards the level crossing, with the 15-ton weighbridge No. 524 and office provided in 1913 on the left and the rendered brick crossing keeper's house built in 1930. The concrete block and tiebars used in the siding were introduced on the GWR in 1943. J. H. RUSSELL

William Piper spent his morning dealing with the goods traffic which arrived on the previous day's stopping goods train. The coal wharfage was held by the South Wales and Cannock Chase Coal Company, which received supplies from Nuneaton. One of the local users who ordered a wagon of coal was William Peachey who had a smallholding tied to The Chequers Inn at Churchill. He would pull up in an 'Oxfordshire' horse-drawn wagon, frequently taking a load up to the village school.

Kingham Hill School, formerly the Kingham Hill Homes, required large quantities of coal. In the early 1930s Bob Hall lived in one of the newly converted outbuildings which had formerly belonged to Churchill Mill. Marjorie recalls "He was always coming up" to collect coal and other goods traffic for Kingham Hill.

A highlight of the day was the 7.40 a.m. Swansea–Newcastle express which passed Sarsden Halt around 12.05 p.m. Marjorie remembers "We had to have the gates open for that. We didn't dare keep them waiting or we would have copped it!"

William Piper and the crew of the stopping goods train. The driver, Harry Butler, worked the turn until c.1940. William Piper's daughter Marjorie remembered that he once gave her a birthday present. The arrival of the goods train must have been quite exciting for Marjorie as a young girl. As she recalled: "They used to take me for rides on that engine while they shunted". This photograph was taken c.1930 after cutbacks in the company required William Piper to work a 16-hour shift from 6.0 a.m. to 10.0 p.m.

The morning shift ended at 2.0 p.m. when William Piper booked off duty, making sure that the signal box was clean. The late-turn duty was carried out by Arthur Bunting, who arrived on a motorcycle fitted with a sidecar. He worked the 2.0–10.0 p.m. shift.

Just after 4.0 p.m. the Newcastle–Swansea express passed through, closely followed by the 4.15 Chipping Norton–Kingham passenger train which stopped at 4.20 p.m.

Although the express was never scheduled to stop at Sarsden Halt, there were instances of it pulling up at least to set down passengers in response to a pre-arranged booking, which was required to be made at least twenty-four hours in advance. Mr. Putman, a ropemaker who kept a shop on Top Side, Chipping Norton, described an arrangement

Another view of the halt on the same spring evening in 1947 with the little weighbridge in the foreground. The cramped yard alongside the original Sarsden siding was enlarged c.1927 when the purchase of extra land allowed wagons to be unloaded along the full length of the loop siding. The timber-framed loading gauge seen in earlier views was evidently not renewed whenever the post expired. J. H. RUSSELL

A better glimpse of the pollarded willows growing alongside the Cornwell or Swailsford Brook. 12th June 1956. S. FLETCHER

whereby if a passenger was travelling from beyond Leicester, it was permissible for him to ask for the train to set down at Sarsden Halt. Mr. Putman used to enquire on the previous day if a train would be stopping at Sarsden Halt, and if so he would board it at Chipping Norton and disembark at Sarsden. Unscheduled stops were definitely not encouraged.

The next train was the 4.03 Banbury–Kingham passenger service which stopped at 4.59, arriving at Kingham at 5.04 p.m. The train returned on its way back to Banbury at 5.11 p.m., then at about 5.37 the Banbury–Kingham pick-up goods arrived. Any traffic for Sarsden was put off but it is not clear whether outgoing wagons were collected at this time, or left at the opposite end of the siding for collection when the train was on its way back from Kingham, calling around 6.56 p.m. Goods items from the roadside van were locked in the signal box.

As part of the economies of the late 1920s, one of the porter posts at Sarsden was abolished and Arthur Bunting transferred away to become a signalman at Bruern Crossing 1½ miles south of Kingham station. William and his wife continued to cover the crossing keeper's duty, the siding and the halt between the hours of 6.0 a.m. and 10.0 p.m.

For the time being, William was still walking the 1½ miles between Kingham and Sarsden Halt at the beginning and end of the day, but in 1930 a new crossing keeper's house (authorised in October 1929) was completed and William and his family moved in so that at least they were on site when they were needed. The details are no longer clear but at one time Horace Duester travelled out from Kingham around 2.0 p.m. to help out for an hour or so and it seems that William's wife covered the crossing keeper's duties at the beginning and end of each day.

In 1930, when Fred Warren was a 16-year-old junior porter at Chipping Norton, he remembers cycling from his home in Bledington to Sarsden Halt to assist with the loading of milk churns on the first train from there to Kingham. Milk for London was brought to the halt by a Mr. Webb using a pony and trap. He worked on behalf of Churchill Farm. The churns were usually of the 17-gallon variety and Fred became quite an expert in rolling them. Apparently, Mrs. Piper was usually either on the early turn or just covered the start of the day and, being unable to handle the 17-gallon churns, Fred went along to deal with them and recalls "The problem was that Mrs. Piper couldn't roll the milk churns or lift the milk onto the train when it came along, so they knew I lived at Bledington and they made me go to Sarsden Halt first. I had to cycle to Sarsden Halt, help put the bloody milk in and then get on the train and come to Chippy. I extended my lunch break to make up for the earlier start." He left his bike at Sarsden either in the waiting shed or under the box steps, and when he caught the late-afternoon train home, he collected the bike and cycled home. It is not clear how the milk was dealt with on Sundays but Fred thinks that

An early view taken at Sarsden Halt of porter Thomas Lee between two unidentified young men. Thomas Lee was born in 1850 in Redmarley, Worcestershire. According to the Churchill census for 1891, he was married with six children and described as a railway porter. COLLECTION ALAN WATKINS

When Fred Warren relieved for Charlie and Annie Hall one summer Sunday in 1935, he took his 17-year-old girlfriend Hilda Bench along for the day. Hilda remembers "It was a Sunday and there was an excursion to Weston-super-Mare due to pass. Fred was there to open the gates." This picture of her on the signal box steps was taken that day.

it went on a service from Banbury to Notgrove and back which was referred to as 'The Milk Train'. "We lost the milk traffic when the dairy opened at Moreton-in-Marsh – it was then collected by road and taken there."

Besides villagers from Churchill, passengers using Sarsden Halt also included staff and pupils of Kingham Hill School. Marjorie recalls that the halt was very busy when the Chipping Norton annual hospital carnival took place. Up to 300 tickets could be sold to visitors.

William Piper kept the halt in good order, not least for the weekly inspections of David Davis, the Chipping Norton station master. Also in the tradition of so many railwaymen, William was a keen gardener who took pride in the allotment gardens behind the platform. When he retired in 1934 at the age of 65, the family moved into a council house in Churchill. He died in 1953 aged 84 and was buried in Churchill cemetery, close to Sarsden Halt.

The entrance gate to the siding, seen here c.1960. J. H. MOSS

The blue-brick signal box housing 11 levers was opened in 1893 but was reduced to ground frame status from 7th March 1899 when a new 6-lever 5½in stud frame was installed. The new frame controlled the gate locks, up and down distant signals and the crossover giving access to the west end of the siding. The building followed a standard GWR design classified by the Signalling Record Society as Type 6. J. R. BATTS

A view of the ground behind the platform c.1950 showing the fence and gate enclosing the vegetable allotment. The three-storey building across the road was the miller's house. J. H. RUSSELL

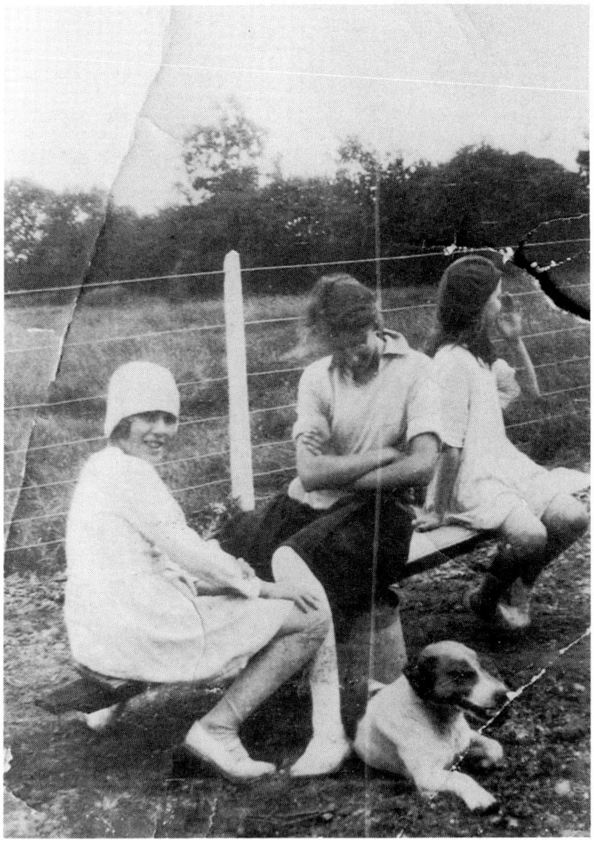

Marjorie Piper recalled often paddling in the brook and playing in the "nice fields, behind the mill, by the railway track". Here we see her friends from Kingham School on a makeshift see-saw, beside the railway, with Roger the dog, c.1930.
CTY. MRS. M. HOWELLS

Charlie Hall and his wife Annie moved into the crossing cottage and took over the responsibility for the crossing and halt. Charlie's main duties were at Kingham, but he also served as a relief porter at Chipping Norton. His brother Harold says "It was worked very much like Rollright on a middle-turn basis from 9.0 a.m. to 6.0 p.m. with an hour for lunch."

The crossing keeper's position was particularly routine, so one night during the early 1930s after Charlie and Annie Hall had finished their duty and gone to sleep, they were unpleasantly surprised to be woken by an engine whistle. It was around 1.0 a.m. and came from an excursion train which they had forgotten was due, and was waiting to be let through the crossing.

Charlie Hall did not remain long at Sarsden Halt. He was transferred to Malvern Link, eventually returning to the area where he served as a relief passenger guard on the Oxford–Worcester line.

During the Second World War, Len Organ was the porter in charge and Cecil Hall assisted. Les Floyd, who spent many years at Kingham Hill, said that Sarsden Halt was very busy during the war years, particularly with the handling of coal traffic.

The duties of Sarsden Halt during its later years were covered by Mr. & Mrs. Loxton, who had previously lived and worked in the West Country.

GEORGE ILIFFE STOKES

Looking towards Kingham from the end of the platform in 1947. The signal on the other side of the level crossing was the down distant for Churchill Crossing about a quarter of a mile further on.

J. H. RUSSELL

M. J. ESAU

The little brick hut on the left dated from the days of the original Sarsden siding. It is seen here from a departing train on 7th April 1962 after the removal of the timber lean-to apparent in the photo below.

An earlier photo taken on 24th April 1955 showing the old brickwork in close-up and the standard GWR halt time-table board which in 1906 was originally mounted on a timber post adjacent to the entrance gate.

J. R. BATTS

CHURCHILL CROSSING 86m 19c

Churchill Crossing c.1930 viewed from the Kingham East down distant signal, looking towards Sarsden Halt. The crossing house had three bedrooms, but the rest of the original layout is not clear. It was built into the side of an embankment, and this produced a large cellar underneath, which was entered through a hatch in the front room. Inside the cottage was a bell indicating the communication between the signal boxes at Chipping Norton West and Kingham East to warn the keeper of an approaching train. The brick structure of the cottage was porous and the internal walls suffered with damp penetration. Around 1918 the company added a cladding of red clay tiles to the walls to alleviate the problem.
COLLECTION ALAN BRAIN

THE point at which the railway crossed the road which runs between Churchill and Kingham came to be known as Churchill Crossing. The road was parallel to Mill Lane which led to Sarsden Halt, and the two crossings were within sight of each other. They were the only manned level crossings on the eastern section of the Banbury & Cheltenham Railway.

When originally built in 1855, it was known as Kingham Crossing and the first known crossing keeper was William Dickens who, born at Bledington in 1813, held the post from 1857. He and his wife had seven children, the last three being born at Churchill. William died in 1894, the inscription on his gravestone at Churchill reading 'For thirty-eight years a railway official at the Kingham Crossing'.

The next crossing keeper was Thomas Wilkins Leadbetter who had been a porter at Fairford. He and his family remained there until March 1906 when he died at the age of 59.

The name 'Kingham Crossing' was changed to 'Churchill Crossing' around this time and the next keeper was Arthur George Watkins. Born at Aston in 1878, he had been working at Paddington Goods Depot when he lost a leg through an accident with a runaway wagon. The GWR fitted him with a false leg and, when he married Alice Eamer in June 1906, the couple were given the position at Churchill.

The Watkins family remained at the crossing for 28 years but as the little lodge was rather cramped for the couple and their six children, the three boys slept at Arthur's mother's house, which she had bought in Kingham Road, Churchill in 1922.

The level crossing gates were run into at various times, Ivor Townsend, signal-

This early 1930s photo of the Watkins family and friends shows (from left to right) back row: Frances, Jim, Eve, unknown, Betty, Arthur, Alice, unknown, unknown; front row: Barbara and Peter.
CTY. MRS. BARBARA SEIDEL

The express train seen against the backdrop of a rural branch line. The westbound 'Ports-to-Ports' approaching Churchill Crossing on a summer afternoon in the 1920s, at about 4.15 p.m.

Arthur Watkins leaning on one of the levers at Churchill Crossing. This view also shows the back of the nameboard. At the far left we can see the small extension added to the north-east side of the lodge which contained the wash-house. Arthur and his family looked after Churchill Crossing for twenty-eight years. He worked to within a few weeks of his death in 1934.

man at Kingham West box, recalling "They'd been knocked down three or four times by trains that would overshoot the signal." One May during the 1920s, a fully-loaded dray, on its way from Hitchmans Brewery in Chipping Norton to Stow Fair, was crossing the line when a light engine from Kingham smashed through the gates, taking the dray up the line and leaving the horse standing in the shafts. The drayman was unhurt but the dray was destroyed and, as Arthur's son Alan explained, "There were marbles everywhere from all the lemonade bottles". They were collected up and apparently buried beside one of the signals.

The gates were normally closed across the railway but at some time during the evening, they were closed across the road. This allowed the passage of any ironstone trains and perhaps the last auto-car without disturbing Arthur's rest. However, he still had to be available to let any road traffic over the line and at some time in the 1920s he rigged up a bell push which rang a bell in the lodge to wake him up to open the gates.

Arthur's duties included refuelling the lamps, including those of the distant signals. He fetched the paraffin from Sarsden Halt and was allowed to draw two gallons at a time. Unofficially, he also used to collect dandelion heads for one of the enginemen for winemaking.

Mr Putman, a Churchill resident, recalled that in the mornings Arthur used to hand his shopping basket and money to

Barbara posing on a motorbike. Apparently, on an occasion when Arthur Watkins could not get both gates open in time, the passing train clipped one of them which swung round, a splintered fragment dislodging one of the crossing lodge tiles. This was a source of conversation among family and friends for many years.

Left: *Barbara, Minnie Howard, a friend of Alice, and Arthur Watkins outside the crossing cottage c.1930.* Right: *The Watkins' dog which was run over by a train and killed.*

Arthur Watkins kept pigs in the sties behind the cottage. Pigs were a valuable food source for those with room to keep them.

Barbara and her grandmother, Alice Watkins.

the fireman of the auto-car who, in turn, gave it to the Chipping Norton station master who would send one of his porters into the town. Arthur's shopping was delivered to him on the next down train.

The crossing keeper's post was not for everyone and, when Arthur was ill in 1934, there was no queue of volunteers to stand in for him. Fred Warren recalled "You were there from morning till night and never got anything for it – no over-time." He was advised to tell the inspector, who was trying to arrange cover, that he didn't know the job. He did this and was asked how long he would need to learn it. "I said a week – and I never did go – George Stayt did it. Mr. Watkins died a few weeks later."

Churchill Crossing was not served by any regular keepers during the war years, but William Cooke and his wife started shortly afterwards and stayed until closure nineteen years later. There is a remarkable sense of continuity at Churchill Crossing witnessed through the careers of just four crossing keepers and their families across a time span of nearly 100 years. This is made all the more poignant by the fact that of all the places on the B&CR, Churchill Crossing changed the least and remains to this day.

Barbara with Teddy c.1930-1.

Barbara Watkins and Alma Ferris photographed on the track at Churchill Crossing c.1929. Although they look extremely vulnerable, they were quite safe under the watchful eye of their grandparents Arthur and Alice Watkins.

KINGHAM 84m 59c

This 1950s photo shows a Cheltenham train signalled for departure over the western part of the Banbury & Cheltenham Railway. Kingham station and the other stations along the route, including Cheltenham St. James, are covered in the next volume.

E. K. LOCKSTONE